# PROPHETIC VOICE NOW

## Crafting Space for Visionary Thinking and Practice

*Rich Murphy*

# Prophetic Voice Now

**Crafting Space for Visionary Thinking and Practice**

---

*Rich Murphy*

First published in 2020
as part of the New Directions in the Humanities Book Imprint
http://doi.org/10.18848/978-1-86335-195-9/CGP  (Full Book)

BISAC Codes:LIT014000, PHI040000, EDU040000

Common Ground Research Networks
2001 South First Street, Suite 202
University of Illinois Research Park
Champaign, IL
61820

Copyright © Rich Murphy 2020

All rights reserved. Apart from fair dealing for the purposes of study, research, criticism or review as permitted under the applicable copyright legislation, no part of this book may be reproduced by any process without written permission from the publisher.

Library of Congress Cataloging-in-Publication Data

Names: Murphy, Rich, 1950- author.
Title: Prophetic voice now : crafting space for visionary thinking and
   practice  / Rich Murphy.
Description: Champaign : Common Ground Research Networks, 2020. | Includes
   bibliographical references. | Summary: "To challenge the
   (self-)alienating and disempowering effects of ideology-driven
   illusions, Rich Murphy's often provocative voice blends three dominant
   streams of enquiry: updating and re-affirming the old Blakean ideal of
   "Giving a body to Falsehood"; advocating a post-symbolic kind of poetic
   fashioning that favors only temporary patterns of understanding over
   fixed and inherited cultural associations; and passionately defending
   the right to a literary/philosophical education as well as the formative
   role of poetry and the arts on the path to overcoming our self-made or
   internalized mental prisons. Contemplating the contingencies of the
   future, the essays collected here may no longer share the confidence of
   Walt Whitman's "So Long!", but they nevertheless hold on to its
   announcement of "a life that shall be copious, vehement, spiritual,
   bold." Therefore, whether one agrees or disagrees with some of Murphy's
   challenging ideas, his essays offer precious mentorship and
   encouragement to any individuals refusing their creative spirit and
   existential self-promise to be crushed"-- Provided by publisher.
Identifiers: LCCN 2020007220 (print) | LCCN 2020007221 (ebook) | ISBN
   9781863351935 (hardback) | ISBN 9781863351942 (paperback) | ISBN
   9781863351959 (pdf)
Subjects: LCSH: Poetics. | Poetry, Modern--21st century--History and
   criticism--Theory, etc.Poetry | Creation (Literary, artistic, etc.) |
   Postmodernism.
Classification: LCC PN1042 .M87 2020  (print) | LCC PN1042  (ebook) | DDC
   814/.6--dc23
LC record available at https://lccn.loc.gov/2020007220
LC ebook record available at https://lccn.loc.gov/2020007221

Cover Photo Credit: Sebastian Palomino pexels-photo-1853373.jpeg

*For Bonnie and for her love*

# Table of Contents

Introduction ..................................................................................................... 1

Chapter Summaries ........................................................................................ 3

Chapter 1 ......................................................................................................... 7
Vanishing Artist: American Poet and Differend

Chapter 2 ....................................................................................................... 17
Reading Wisdoms

Chapter 3 ....................................................................................................... 25
Spectacle and Aporia in Ted Kooser and John Ashbery

Chapter 4 ....................................................................................................... 37
The Hopkins Path to Postmodern Poetry

Chapter 5 ....................................................................................................... 49
"Vexed to Nightmare by a Rocking Cradle": Ginsberg's Performativity

Chapter 6 ....................................................................................................... 59
McLuhan's Warning, Frye's Strategy, Emerson's Dream

Chapter 7 ....................................................................................................... 67
Poetry's Evolving Ecology: Toward a Post-Symbol Landscape

Chapter 8 .............................................................................................................. 77
Living Culture/Reading Poetry

Chapter 9 .............................................................................................................. 93
Prophetic Voice Now

Chapter 10 .......................................................................................................... 103
The Acts of a Solitary Thinker and the Fragile Absolute: A Case Study

Epilogue ............................................................................................................. 117
Interregnum: Capitalism in Crisis

Acknowledgements ............................................................................................ 121

# Introduction

This collection of essays dates back at least 20 years and contains a few threads for consideration: Education and the importance of self-education for those interested in the arts today are highlighted in "Vanishing Artist" and "McLuhan's Warning, Frye's Strategy, Emerson's Dream." Breaking frames with new reasoning is explored in "Reading Wisdom." Modern and postmodern poetics are explored in "Spectacle in Aporiain Ted Kooser and John Ashbery," "The Hopkins Path to Postmodern Poetry," and "Poetry's Evolving Ecology: Toward a Post-Symbol Landscape." Our prophetic moment in history is explained in "'Vexed to Nightmare by a Rocking Cradle:' Ginsberg's Performativity," "Living Culture: Reading poetry," "Prophetic Voice Now." When writing of the arts, I am writing on the art of poetry. However, it may be read as a synecdoche.

The limits of capitalism are its inability, for the most part, to commodify the arts, leaving it subject to contingent forces that could eliminate it altogether. Other limits include the limits of the "educated" masses they are unable or unwilling to open to and experience arts. There is an unwillingness to try to explore outside the limits of the debt driven consumer's money worship. It is here that education has let democracy down.

The collection also gives witness to the decline in the arts and education, not necessarily art education alone but certainly liberal art education. It is my belief that art is so essential to education that responsible societies wish to produce intellectually and emotionally mature adults for decision making in a democracy: Thus my beginning with an early essay "Vanishing Artist." Of course, there are factor that interrupt the education of young people and we may not have produced a society that is truly interested in the value of art in education. Though I have been told that there are some societies that are doing a fair job at it, the USA does not seem, has not seemed interested in achieving a society of literate, self-actualized, responsible adults. So, even at the level of education, democracy here is one of façade as it representational model is now owned by corporations. We can witness this in the attempt to merge the department of education with the department of labor.

With the essays "Vanishing Artist" and "McLuhan's Warning, Frye's Strategy, Emerson's Dream" the education component of the book is covered for the most part. "Reading Wisdoms" demonstrates how outside reasoning disrupts understanding whether in "folk wisdom" or higher culture poetry while it demonstrates the reasoning in the selections for examination. This essay prepares the way for postmodern poetics that will be found in "Spectacle in Aporiain Ted Kooser and John Ashbery," "The Hopkins Path to Postmodern Poetry," and "Poetry's Evolving Ecology: Toward a Post-Symbol Landscape."

In these essays, the writer attempts to highlight the differences and progression toward a postmodern poetics. While the first of these three contrasts modern and postmodern poetics, the second essay asserts a pathway via Gerard Manley Hopkins desperation (not unlike Van Gogh's) to maintaining the relationship between art and religion culminates in writers of projectivist verse and poets such as John Ashbery and Arthur Vogelsang. With pathways in mind the third essay wonders whether there might be and how one might achieve a post-symbol landscape for poetry. In that essay poems by Jorie Graham and Charles Bernstein are considered.

Since the writing of the last essay, the issues became clearer to me with the 2008 financial crash and the recognition and implications of our Anthropocene planet. Both have brought about what Zygmunt Bauman calls an interregnum, a contingent time to consider change. Having read Daniel Dennett's work and in particular Yuval Noah Harari's provocations in his two books on "history" of our species, my writing in both poetry and prose has been affected. It is a time to attempt not only to save writing and reading from McLuhan's warning but a time to perhaps influence the direction that seems all too inevitable.

"'Vexed to Nightmare by a Rocking Cradle:' Ginsberg's Performativity," "Living Culture: Reading poetry," "Prophetic Voice Now" and "The Fragile Absolute: A Case Study" close this book with a call for writers practice craft to follow Marshall McLuhan's and Richard Rorty's maxims about writing for the future. We have nothing to lose. I first consider a recent prophet voice in Allen Ginsberg's "Howl," examining where I believe it succeeds and fails as a prophetic voice and prophetic poem. The second essay in this grouping examines what I contend is the demise of literary poetry and the triumph of capitalist poetry. I end the essay suggesting that it is time to fall in love with a new ideology as suggested by Slavoj Žižek. The third essay is a rationale for and the actual call for prophetic voice in writing as a way to redirect the seeming inevitable. Finally, the last essay is autobiographical in an attempt to demonstrate Žižek's concept of the "fragile absolute" in a more personal setting. My hope is to draw an outline of an alternative to Homo Deus and the-internet-of-all-things by responding to the spiritual wound, and to suggest a way forward not only for young (readers and) writers but for the cultural voices as a whole. Yes, voices count now.

CHAPTER SUMMARIES

**1. Vanishing Artist:** This essay chronicles the decline in the funding for American education at a time when it was needed most. Neo-liberal policies and TINA were taking hold at the time of writing the essay. The essay also addresses how poetry and the arts were attempting to address the cultural issues of the day and how the causes of those issues were suppressing the artistic education and expression. References include Charles Olson, John Ashbery, Joseph Brodsky, Jean-Francois Lyotard, and Richard Gray.

**2. Reading Wisdoms:** This essay explains how important knowing critical and cultural theory is for a contemporary poet. The writer explores the idea of generation mentioned within Mick Jagger's "As Tears Go By," W.B. Yeats' "Sailing to Byzantium," and Gayatri Chakravorty Spivak's "Reading the World." He establishes a connection within each as the essay moves through each work's passages on the idea of generation. The essay equates wisdom to Michele Foucault's "empirical order of a primary code" and the "middle region which liberates order itself" to the place for poetry and what Jean-Francois Lyotard would call the differend. The essay seems to suggest that the idea of "poetic truth" is more difficult to access than one might think. The essay closes with the writer suggesting the kinds of reading and thinking contemporary poets should be doing in light of the thinking brought to bear in the late 20$^{th}$ and early 21$^{st}$ Century. This essay prepares the reader for later essays.

**3. Spectacle and Aporia in Ted Kooser and John Ashbery:** The essay recognizes Jacques Derrida's understanding of the idea of a non-transcendental sublime (aporia) and explores the difference between aporia and Roland Barthe's idea of "spectacle of excess." The paper will acknowledge that the dichotomy is false but credible. This author will then use the two lenses to analyze poems by Ted Kooser who is considered one of America's most popular poets and John Ashbery who is considered by many critics to be the most important poet writing in English today. This author finds that as poetry becomes Modern and familiar, it becomes a thing of beauty and a spectacle of excess. When it is postmodern, it is a spectacle of the sublime.

**4. The Hopkins Path to Postmodern Poetry:** This essay asserts that the poetics of New England poet Denise Levertov may be seen as a bridge from Victorian poet Gerard Manley Hopkins' poetics to postmodern poetics of today. Using the imagism and the ideas of Richard Rorty, William Pratt, Jean-Francois Lyotard, Charles Bernstein, and Bob Perelman, the writer outlines how the key concepts of imagism were adopted from Gerard Manley Hopkins and in new guises used by modernist poets such as Ezra Pound and Denise Levertov and postmodern poets such as Sheila Murphy and Arthur Vogelsang. The writer also contends that what governs the changes in the Victorian poet's desperate poetics is attitude: Modernist poetry is one of mourning, and postmodernist poetry is one of joy in the absurd.

**5. "Vexed to Nightmare by a Rocking Cradle": Ginsberg's Performativity**: This essay examines Ginsberg's written performance that is "Howl" to assess its strengths and weaknesses as a modern and postmodern poetic work and as a tool for exploring Ginsberg's creative mind. This writer asserts that the poem could have been a powerful poem on the margins of the symbolic order indicting patriarchy and perhaps its links to the Fuehrer and fascism. However, because of its premature birth, or its rushed performance in its writing, Ginsberg (who one would think would be at home on the margins) at best targets housewives, an easy target, in a poem uneasy in its own skin.

To construct context for the performativity of the poem and for its writer as an icon performing his life, the paper attempts to recreate the cultural background that gave birth to both. The paper describes the background after America's victory of World War II. It explains how that setting prepared American culture and the poetry world for the appearance of his personality and poetry in spite of the McCarthy era and the Cold War. My paper explains how Allen Ginsberg made history and how history made Allen Ginsberg. It will examine how the postwar American psyche created the rebel phenomenon and how Ginsberg's performativity prepared a way to liberate the American psyche. While Ginsberg's attempt to destabilize privileged gender roles fails in his visionary intent during the performance of writing the poem, it succeeds in his performance of his life. The poem seems to stumble upon a major postmodern imperative, "presenting the unpresentable."

**6. McLuhan's Warning, Frye's Strategy, Emerson's Dream:** This essay reminds the reader of McLuhan's warning about the effects of digital media and globalism, reminds the reader of the value of the artist, reminds the reader about the need for Frye's educated imagination to assist the artist and the citizen, and reminds the reader of Emerson's dream for the United States of America. It connects the "doctrines" of the three writers to highlight the failure to live up to them. McLuhan warned that the artists know how to manage the radical changes in society. Frye advocated the strategy for every literate citizen in a democracy: Educate the imagination. Emerson projected for the USA precisely what these other two thinkers spoke to in his essays.

**7. Poetry's Evolving Ecology: Toward a Post-Symbol Landscape:** According to this meditative essay, the shifting of Western poetics from Modernism to Postmodernism is evolutionary, and formative imagination's function in that shifting is to serve as a resource for contingency. According to his thinking poetics and ecology are influenced by globalization. The meditation explores the shedding of cultural symbols in poetry baring the more contingent language of signifiers. It suggests that the resulting ecology of signifiers brings readers closer to nature because it removes assumed values of the culture. The result is postmodern approaches to poetry. The essay outlines the relationship between the formative imagination and contingency. It remarks on how the nature of mediation and the formative imagination pivot on contingency allowing poetics to adjust to perpetual change. It also recognizes that the signifier and aporia have become basic tools of the poetic imagination marking time until multiculturalism has established itself and perhaps a new world literature becomes one language. The meditation uses a poem by Jorie Graham as an example of poetry bridging the religious symbolism to Darwinian thought. Charles Bernstein's poem, stripped of cultural symbolism, is an example of a poem of contingency. Together, they illustrate the evolution of poetics and its most contemporary ecology. The meditation concludes with the poet highlighting the changing ecology in his own poetry from cultural to multicultural symbolism and then to the threshold of contingency.

**8. Living Culture: Reading Poetry:** The essay argues in five sections that because literary poetry wasn't read and known by Americans, capitalist poetry took its place, the poetry of the advertisement. The argument is made that the suppression of art and poetry from contention of a possible ideology leaves capitalist poetry as the background ideology only. References are made to Herbert Marcuse, Theodor Adorno, Neil Postman, Noam Chomsky, Zygmunt Bauman, and Slavoj Žižek among others in order to support Northrop Frye's contention for an educated imagination. Further, the essay argues that because of the under-developed skills that an educated imagination provides, our society will suffer the emotional abuse of behaviorist, cyber-technicians, and government officials in their herding techniques of the future. Finally, the essay argues that the failure of our culture to educate the imagination has led to the downfall of the Enlightenment providing a lacuna or end to our love affair with capitalism where we could fall in love again with a new ideology. The essay follows Bernay's capitalist poetry and outlines the reasons for the demise of literary poetry. It gives two examples of capitalist poetry and how each functions and gives three examples of mainstream literary poetry and how they function.

**9. Prophetic Voice Now:** This essay argues why the prophetic voice in fiction and poetry writers is so important now. Given that our global and national cultures are interregnum at this time and that we are at the threshold of such phenomena as the-internet-of-all-things and transhumans (or what Harari calls Homo Deus), the essay explains why giving voice to alternative myths may help redirect the current direction so that humans value their being, their becoming, lives as Nietzsche's acrobats. The essay refers to Harari, Žižek, Sloterdijk, Heidegger, and others in its argument for prophetic voices.

**10. The Fragile Absolute: A Case Study:** This essay is an autobiographical "case study" in an attempt to map what Žižek calls "the fragile absolute" personally as the destination of Joseph Campbell's "follow your bliss," the Heideggerian becoming, and Maslow's climb to "self-actualization"(and self-realization) in Sloterdijk's praxis of culture's and humanity's immune system for Homo sapiens. The writer sees the spirit responding to its wound via compensation as members of the fragile absolute, a way forward for Homo sapiens.

*Prophetic Voice Now*

**Epilogue** Interregnum: Capitalism in Crisis: An image representing our situation and the two directions for the future. One direction represents our default and one advocated by this writer's prophetic voice. An explanation follows.

CHAPTER 1

# Vanishing Artist: American Poet and Differend

> "[I]n the end democracy diverts the imagination from all that is external to man and fixes it on man alone."
> (Alexis de Tocqueville, 1840)

> **The Hermit Cackleberry Brown, on Human Vanity:**
>
> caint call your name
> but your face is easy
>
> come sit
>
> now some folks figure theyre
> betten
> cowflop they
> aint
>
> not a bit
>
> just good to hold the world together
> like hooved up ground
>
> that's what (257)
>
> (Jonathan Williams, 1982)

As I was beginning to write this essay, I was reading Czeslaw Milosz's book *The Witness of Poetry,* and his essay "Poets and the Human Family" was of particular interest to me. I had been cataloging the various layers of alienation of the American poet from his/her human family and attempting to understand the reasons for them, beginning with existential alienation and moving outward to cultural alienation. In the essay he tells us that "... poets in the Twentieth Century are by nature isolated, deprived of a public, 'unrecognized,' while the great soul of the people is asleep, unaware of itself ..." He goes on to state:

> This raises the issue of the poets' anxiety, the anxiety that has seized them every time they have encountered the man in the street: at such moments they have sensed their own refinement, their "culture," which has made them incomprehensible; thus they have felt potentially subject to the mockery of

the common man, who found their occupation unmanly. When they have tried to ingratiate themselves with him by "lowering themselves to his level," the results were not good for poetry does not accord with such forced operations (30).

Milosz's explanation for the poet's isolation seems too simple. Milosz blames poets in this essay and suggests that during the Nazi's occupation of Poland that poetry became "as essential as bread" (31). Poetry becoming as essential as bread may have had as much to do with the changing political paradigm of the "man in the street" as with the poets. In a democracy, the great sleeping soul of the people cannot be let off the hook completely. I am not convinced that elitism and modernity are the poles separating the poet from his/her audience. There is a responsibility of an educated democracy to bring balance to itself and to foster paralogy. We learn early in a democracy that it demands that its citizens be literate in order for them participate fully. It was the idea of an educated democracy that inspired Joseph Brodsky lecturing at the Library of Congress to remark, "there is now a discernible opportunity to turn this nation into an enlightened democracy." (Stephenson, *The Atlantic Monthly*)

Joseph Campbell approaches the problem of the alienation of the poet from his/her culture more dynamically with the idea of democracy in mind and to my mind has a clearer understanding of the situation. According to Campbell in his book, *Hero with a Thousand Faces,* the artist is the creative citizen who journeys inward and returns with something vital to relate to the culture. He ends his book calling for the democratic ideal:

> The modern hero, the modern individual who dares to heed the call and seek the mansion of that presence with whom it is our whole destiny to be atoned, cannot, indeed must not, wait for his community to cast off its slough of pride, fear, rationalized avarice, and sanctified misunderstanding. "Live," Nietzsche says, "as though the day were here." It is not society that is to guide and save the creative hero, but precisely the reverse. And so, every one of us shares the supreme ordeal—carries the cross of the redeemer—not in the bright moments of his tribe's great victories, but in the silences of his personal despair. (391)

Campbell attempts to include what Milosz would call a newly awakened public. His book suggests that existential alienation may be a metanarrative for every educated citizen. This metanarrative may be of value by leading us away from the political notions of the bohemians regarding the bourgeoisie at the dawn of modernity and toward the idea that the artist returns to the culture with something vital, the unconventional possibilities. He goes as far as to suggest that the citizen must be an artist and vice versa. The idea may be one for our dreams, and for so many reasons, its realization unlikely. However, Campbell's call is an attractive goal that could resolve the alienation of the American artist. The poet travels inward away from the conventions of his/her culture and then returns with insights and possible new, more genuine, conventions for the culture of his/her time. The insights and conventions of the poet are meant to bring the experience of being alive to any who recognize the value of that experience. Following Campbell's implication, if every citizen aspired to be a kind of artist, perhaps the culture could renew itself person by person.

I am interested in examining the layers of alienation faced by poets to see whether I may expose subtleties in their situation and how we may progress from Milosz's understanding of the relationship of the poet and the human family to Campbell's understanding of it. I wish to define what I am calling existential alienation, social alienation, marketplace alienation, political alienation, and cultural alienation, and then examine Jean-Francois Lyotard's concept of the "differend" as it applies to poets. I use the term "layers" to imply metaphorically my sense of being an amateur archeologist. By differend, I mean a person active in his/her alienation through the process of freeing oneself of coercion, suspecting every perspective, arresting performativity, and interrogating discourse while practicing paralogy. (Rothbone) For poets it means "invoking the unpresentable in presentation itself, that which refuses the consolation of correct forms, refuses the consensus of taste permitting a common experience of nostalgia for the impossible, and inquires into new presentations – not to take pleasure in them, but to better produce the feeling that there is something unpresentable. (Lyotard 15)

The first layer of alienation an American poet endures is existential, a psychological point of view. One might think of a poet's alienation as represented by a cyclical journey that produces two preverbal polar utterances or impulses: "I am very lonely," and "I just want to be alone." The first preverbal utterance is one of solipsism, whereupon the poet begins to reach out to an audience with his/her art to offer an experience of the sublime. The second preverbal utterance is from recognition of the limitation of the experience. Both utterances are profound in that they bring the artist through the regenerative cycle of creativity to encounter the sublime: loneliness inspires the poet; the desire to be alone withdraws the poet. The cycle of existential alienation is at the core of his/her existence. From that cycle comes a body of work from that poet's lifetime.

When the poet has as much success as is possible composing a particular work of art, the audience has the experience of being alive similar to the artist's creative experience. The artist moves the audience through a similar journey as the one he/she had discovered with his/her subject. Works of art bring us to the recognition that the only conventions we have are the ones we make. Marshall McLuhan agrees when he states,

> The function of the artist in correcting the unconscious bias of perception in any given culture can be betrayed if he merely repeats the bias of the culture instead of adjusting it. In fact, it can be said that any culture which feeds merely on its direct antecedents is dying. In this sense the role of art is to create the means of perception by creating counter environments that open the door of perception to people otherwise numbed in a nonperceivable situation. (*Essential McLuhan*, 342)

Recognizing this then allows the citizen the freedom to choose, allowing him/her to be the creator of his/her life.

So it is self-destructive when a society turns on its artists and through fierce neglect denies their existence or regards them as evil. When a society turns on its artists, the artist suffers a social alienation, a second alienation where a society applies the label of "other." Social alienation is a rejection added to the existential withdrawal of the poet. The social alienation of the poet begins with the education in schools, where creative spirits are thwarted if they have survived life in the family from which they are released by day. Public schools are where children become socialized into the culture, yet this is also where alienation begins for the young artist. Too many artists become artists in spite of their education, not because of it.

Democracy's great experiment of educating the masses is an ongoing, dynamic experiment. Each generation amasses its resources and deficits peculiar to that generation in public schools and becomes that generation's contribution to the culture. Schools are where socialization takes place and where values are identified and instilled for each generation. However, the public school system in America from its beginnings has failed to recognize the possible contribution of art in the lives of the students and in the culture as a whole. In a recent article in the *International Journal of Leadership in Education,* Charles J. Fazzaro and James E. Walter summarize the problem stating:

> the current structure of educational policy formation is likely to promote a narrow, homogenous, coerced view of what counts as knowledge. This is 'consensus' achieved through the hegemony of the epistemology of scientific-technical knowledge that has characterized US education for at least 100 years. In short, the bounded scientific-technical knowledge presently at the core of US public school education policy and practices is not adequate to accommodate the wide, if not infinite, spectrum of values in a dynamic, vibrant democratic society. (28)

At this moment in Boston, the Athens of America, because of the state and federal budget crisis, the governor is attempting to sell the nation's only public art college. Art curriculums are the first to suffer cuts or elimination. School districts are laying off teachers and teaching larger classes without supplies. The financial crisis is so desperate that Boston and other cities are selling the sides of buses and walls of school property to advertisers. Spokesman for Boston Public Schools Jonathan Polumbo told the *Boston Globe,* "We were in national publications saying that we didn't want to do this. Then the budget situation hit." He later added, "If ad revenue can plug some holes, I think we have to do it." (Saltzman, B9) A society that can't maintain funding for its schools is a long way from valuing art and democracy for that matter.

Social alienation came with the American Puritan's belief in Secular Calling and the Protestant Ethic. Secular Calling led to the later idea that if in the marketplace one is successful at one's calling, it is a sign that God favors one on Earth. These two ethical values reinforced by their literal interpretation of the Bible developed a value system for the Puritans and their progeny that thought of artists as tools of the devil, alienating them from the social order. This is the heritage and backdrop for any contemporary literary culture in the US. For Nathaniel Hawthorne, one of our first artists, a writer of fiction, the value system complicated the existential alienation in his creative cycle with social, marketplace, and cultural alienation.

The marketplace is the third layer of alienation. Its interest in only what sells has accelerated to the point where conglomerates have purchased literary presses and now don't feel responsible to bring to the literate public something that is not in the mold of the tried and true: "financial success, rather than literary excellence is the goal." Roger Straus of Farrar, Straus, and Giroux speaking of publishing in 1946, puts it this way, "they weren't running their business for large profits. They were interested in good literature. Now, the goal is to get larger. The easiest way to increase the look of your balance sheet is to buy another company." (Hirschberg, 30) Gina Centrello of Random House, where each division is expected to show a 12 percent return on sales, suggests "Instead of feverishly arguing the relative talents of various writers or her love (or hate) of a particular book, she is most anxious about, and fascinated by, what will sell." (Hirschberg, 31) Except for a very limited list of token poets who through its advertising sponsorship may break even financially for the subsidiary, the conglomerates are silent. Today, we have "people" or "working class" poets publishing in small presses or at vanity presses whose books do not sell or even find space on bookstore shelves, just as we have truly "alternative" musicians or classical musicians who will never be heard by the masses and independent movie directors whose films don't make it to the theaters near you. We can say this for all the arts and their tradition in the US. Remember, Whitman published his own poetry.

Not much has changed in other ways since Hawthorne's entertaining post-Bowdoin newspaper *The Spectator* in which he complains "wealth does not lie in the path of literature" and later, tongue in cheek advertises for help: "Employment will be given to any number of indigent poets and authors at this office." (*The Spectator*, Phillips 2000) Then, as now, artists were placed outside the human family. In fact, the marketplace has so alienated the artist that it has gone on the attack. The recent Copyright Extension Act in America extends copyright pre- 1978 for corporate works for 100 years and applies retroactively. Artists of all genres can no longer borrow from these art works to use as symbols in their art without being sued.

Political alienation, the fourth layer, often manifests itself through censorship. An example of the censorship I am referring to is the following. In a recent sermon by Ayatollah Khamenei at Tehran University he declared that anyone who accused the Islamic Republic of despotism was either 'the agent of the enemy, or its dupe.'" (deBellaigue 51) How far away is Khamenei's point from John Ashcroft's warning: "To those who scare peace-loving people with phantoms of lost liberty, my message is this: Your tactics only aid terrorists, for they erode our national unity and diminish our resolve. They give ammunition to America's enemies and pause to America's friends?" (Cohn, 1) The atmosphere of intimidation by Ashcroft underscores a culture that has always struggled with complexity, preferring the simple "us and them" mind set. In despotic regimes the artists are shot. In America poets are starved, ignored until they give it up and find a trade. I suppose American poets should feel lucky.

Before 9/11, censorship was more subtle in its coercion and responded to positively by most citizens, but it was less effective on the poet. After the horror, intimidation works very well via such instruments as "The Patriot Act." Today, many artists censor themselves. Few chance the wrath of a frightened public. In an atmosphere where an American flag on your home and car are the tickets into a civil neighborhood or shopping mall, where mass media spoon feeds its sound bites in such rapid succession any possible question from the pedestrian is unheard and unanswered.

If consciousness is necessary to have a culture, then a culture's artists are its self-conscious agents. If our culture through its families and educational systems merely promotes consciousness and not a consciousness about itself, then the culture is blind to itself and not interested in art, nor is it living up to its educational potential in a democratic society. This may be future what historians identify as the cause of this country to its downfall. Democracy's experiment with education from elementary school systems to college needs to succeed in bringing creativity and art to the center of its agenda. The more people participating in the arts, the healthier, less alienated are artists and individual community members.

When an audience is engaged, or becomes a participant, there is no alienation, and in fact it is the only time that the culture is in communication with itself, creating self-consciousness that may truly see itself as a construct, sees its future possibilities. The audience, "the great soul of the people" identifies with the artist. (Milosz, 30) The artist creates the table around which a culture breaks bread as a family. Without the table and conversation, the culture, lacking self-consciousness, starves, and the poet remains alienated.

However, the postmodern thinker Jean-Francois Lyotard tells us that the postmodern intellectual is active in his/her alienation from society because it is the only way that one can be truly free. He tells us that intellectuals must be free of social coercion, suspect every perspective, interrogate all discourse, and arrest inclinations toward performativity: One must be a differend, "the other." (Rothbone, 3)

At first, the poet wants to embrace the idea of being active in one's alienation as a differend, but to what purpose? Any poet in American culture is an enigma, buried alive in layers of shunning, perhaps already a differend. It is what he/she has been living. Beneath the gravel of the anti-intellectual, anti-artistic community, the idealist dreams that a greater segment of the community in a democracy could be "cosmic dancers," the differends, the others. However, the idealistic, creative intellect in American culture is also active, and if the creative expression of the exploring intellect is to be labeled elitist, then American educators have let the culture down. I believe they have and continue to do so. The poet is alive and self-conscious and can't put him/herself to sleep with 'the great soul of the people.' Understanding his/her self as a construct, he/she must move on and be self-conscious of alienation's ethical dilemmas in doing so.

The differend poet is America's post-modern poet. The differend poet may be a reaction to the layers of alienation put upon poets by the human family in America or may be the movement of poets through the ideas of our time. Any art form is first an arresting of performativity in a culture where reading is done first if not solely for pragmatic purposes. So, any poet today may be closer to the differend than he/she thinks. However, we can read in Projective poetry the writer's exploration of perspectives through the diversity of voices, interrogation of his/her inclination, and the suspicion of discourse in the juxtaposition of his/her words. While the exploration and interrogation causes the reader to contemplate convention, it demands interaction of a willing reader, a reader unlike most today who read little poetry as it is. In fact, we can read in Charles Olson's manifesto his urging fellow poets to move to adopt aspects of the differend.

> A poem is energy transferred from where the poet got it (he will have some several causations), by way of the poem itself to, all the way over to, the reader. . .the poem itself must, at all points, be a high energy-construct and, at all points, an energy-discharge. So: how is the poet to accomplish same energy, how is he, what is the process by which a poet gets in, at all points energy at least the equivalent of the energy which propelled him in the first place, yet an energy which is peculiar to verse alone and which will be, obviously, also different from the energy which the reader, because he is a third term, will take away?...FORM IS NEVER MORE THAN AN EXTENSION OF CONTENT...ONE PERCEPTION MUST IMMEDIATELY AND DIRECTLY LEAD TO A FURTHER PERCEPTION. (148-149)

Richard Grey pastes together Olson's intent in his book *American Poetry of the Twentieth Century*: "the ideal form would consist of a steady, dense stream of perceptions...so that the poem could become more 'the act of the instant' than 'the act of thought about the instant.'" (279) We find in Olson's method Nietzche's perspectivalism, Lyotard's paralogy, and the advocacy of multiple perceptions in an attempt to allow the reader to experience the process of consciousness, a process that questions the conventions of thought. We can find Olsen's Black Mountain influence in the "New York School" and in "language poetry" movement.

John Ashbery is often thought of as from the New York School and as a language poet. In his short poem "Thoughts of a Young Girl," from his book *The Tennis Court Oath* he divides the poem into the thoughts of a young girl and the narrator's thoughts of a young girl. The reader isn't given much prompting of the two kinds of thought. However, we can see by the quotation marks in the poem that these are someone else's words. The reference to "the tower," and the submission of "to show you I'm not mad," (even with its double entendre) and "You were too good to cry much over me" help us hear a woman's voice while "Signed, The Dwarf" cinches the idea of 'the other.' (14) In the second section of the poem there are no quotations, so the reader hears the poem's persona narrate the role of women over the "centuries:" "She always knows / How to be utterly delightful." By calling to the girl (his persona?) "Oh my daughter, / My sweetheart, daughter of my late employer, princess," hurrying her arrival, Ashbery's persona constructs its identity via multiple perspectives and then suggests desire for matriarchy. The poem's lines seem to fold back upon, and almost nullify, themselves, each invoking the unpresentable. The multiple perspectives within each section of the poem, the two perspectives of the sections themselves, the suggestion in the title, and the construction of the poem that reveals the process of consciousness are evidence of the differend in his poem.

### Thoughts of a Young Girl

"It is such a beautiful day I had to write you a letter
from the tower, and to show I'm not mad:
I only slipped on the cake of soap of the air
And drowned in the bathtub of the world.
You were too good to cry much over me.
And now I let you go. Signed, The Dwarf."

I passed by late in the afternoon
And the smile still played about her lips
As it has for centuries. She always knows
How to be utterly delightful. Oh my daughter,
My sweetheart, daughter of my late employer, princess,
May you not be long on the way! (14)

Ashbery is not the only differend. His book *The Tennis Court Oath* did more to promote language poetry than he will acknowledge. If fact, he has mentioned that the book should never have been published. Never the less, it's fair to say that the book is an interesting document for language poets who take Olsen's manifesto, with his idea of composing by "field," seriously in their effort to represent the self as a construct and to reveal the process of consciousness as a venue to remind us that the only conventions we have are the ones we make.

"Do Flies Remember Us" by Jean Valentine is an example of a language poem. It is also the poetry of the differend. It illustrates an interest in process of consciousness and self as a construct and represents again its active alienation, assuming the differend's notions in that it interrogates its own discourse and doubts each perspective it presents.

### Do Flies Remember Us

Do flies remember us
We don't them
We say "fly"
Say
"woman"
"man"

you gone
through my hands
me through your hands

> our footprints feeling
> over us
> thirstily. (170)

Since the beginning of modernism the artists have been comparing themselves to scientists, as though artists were trying to legitimatize themselves. Today, the American poet's and human family's situation may be that of the scientist of quantum mechanics and the citizen. In his recent book *Democracy, Culture and the Voice of Poetry*, Robert Pinsky speaks the obvious when he tells us that there is no place in American culture for poetry (as I do in this essay) and echoes Milosz when he gives voice to the American poet's fear of lost and/or excessive differentiation that embodies an anxiety: "that of being cut off from memory – forgotten…that American poetry is cut off from American culture." Pinsky's Favorite Poem Project is one man's attempt at bridging American Culture to its past poets. For the post-modern American poet and his/her potential audience, however, it is even more extreme. They live in parallel universes, where the poet is invisible to that possible audience, the rest of the human family, the great sleeping soul of the people.

If the situation were a tug-of-war, the human family would be dragging the post-modern poet behind them. If the poets are leaders or those who "hold the world together" as Jonathan Williams suggests in my epigraph, American post-modern poets have left the sleeping soul and have blazed a trail that will not be tracked. I do not think I am overstating the situation. If I am right, and the post-modern poet is also the differend who lives "as thought the day were here," we may not be holding the world together, and we may not be inviting from the democratic masses "the modern individual who dares to heed the call and seek the mansion of that presence with whom it is our whole destiny to be atoned." (Campbell, 391) Should we be?

## WORKS CITED

Ashbery, John. "Thoughts of a Young Girl." *The Tennis Court Oath*. Middletown: Wesleyan University Press, 1962.

Campbell, Joseph. *The Hero with a Thousand Faces*. Princeton: Princeton University Press, 1973.

Cohn, Marjorie. "The Patriotic Duty to Dissent." March 8, 2002. www.marjoriecohn.com/the-patriotic-duty-to-dissent/.

deBellaigue, Christopher. "The Loneliness of the Supreme Leader." *New York Review of Books*, vol. 50, no., 1. Jan. 2003, p. 16.

Fazzaro, Charles J. and James E. White. "Schools for Democracy: Lyotard, Dissensus and Education." *International Journal of Leadership in Education*, vol. 5, no. 1, 2002, pp. 15-32.

Gray, Richard. *American Poetry of the Twentieth Century*. London: Longman, 1990.

Hawthorne, Nathaniel. *Spectator*. Aug. 1820. Salem: Peabody Essex Museum Library Archive.

Hirschberg, Lynn. "Nothing Random." *The New York Times Magazine*. 20 Jul. 2003, pp. 28-66.

Lyotard, Jean-Francois. *The Postmodern Explained*. Minneapolis: University of Minnesota Press, 1992, pp. 1-16.

McLuhan, Marshall. *Essential McLuhan*, edited by Eric McLuhan & Frank Zingrone. Toronto: Anansi, 1995.

Millington, Richard H. "The Meaning of Hawthorne's Women." *Hawthorne in Salem Project,* Jun. 2000. www.hawthorneinsalem.org/.

Milosz, Czeslaw. "Poets and the Human Family." *The Witness of Poetry.* Cambridge: Harvard University Press, 1983.

Olson, Charles. "Projective Verse." *The Poetics of the New American Poetry*, edited by Donald Allen and Warren Tallman, New York: Grove Press, 1973.

Pinsky, Robert. *Democracy, Culture and the Voice of Poetry.* Princeton: Princeton University Press, 2002.

Saltzman, Jonathan. "Taking Ads to School." *Boston Globe,* 8 Jun. 2003.

Stephenson, Wen. "The Matter of Poetry." *The Atlantic Monthly.* 1 Apr. 1996. www.theatlantic.com/unbound/poetry/poetint.htm.

Valentine, Jean. "Do Flies Remember Us." *The Best American Poetry*, edited by Robert Creeley and David Lehman, New York: Scribner, 2002.

Williams, Jonathan. "The Hermit Cackleberry Brown, on Human Vanity:" *The Post-Moderns: The New American Poetry Revisited*, edited by Donald Allen and George F. Butterick. New York: Grove Press, 1982.

CHAPTER 2

## Reading Wisdoms

"The anaesthetic effect of custom being destroyed, I would begin to think and to feel very melancholy things."
(Marcel Proust, 1956)

Wisdom is commonly thought of as an application of a tradition's understanding or knowledge in resolving life's everyday problems in a culture. However, one tradition's wisdom may be a solution or thinking method that is functional in a different culture. Of course, each tradition has its own context for its own wisdom, even though wisdom may be versatile and may deliberately be borrowed to work in another context. There may be a wisdom that transcends all traditions but it would have to have been borrowed and have had a starting point. That kind of wisdom may be connected with the human life-cycle or with what Jung called the collective unconscious. Shared wisdom is probably one culture's problem-solving cross-pollinating to the effect of becoming more universal. However, the particular tool (wisdom) may also be being used for purposes not intended. A hammer becomes a saw and this may account for most of the cross-pollination, the misuse of a tool that probably was even ineffective in the culture of origin.

In the age of globalization, wisdom may be exhausted with wisdoms inter-pollinating, and twisting the wisdoms' intents. Globalization is certainly causing tension in tradition-focused cultures. Science may also be eradicating the whole notion of wisdom. Foreign wisdom may at least call attention to perspectives from folks from other traditions or who are considered on the fringe of a tradition to which they offer perspective. In some cultures in the West tradition is generational at best. Wisdom may be a tall figure that gives comfort to folk or a culture, but it is also pathology of power that allows thinking to stop so that others may control.

When someone from outside or on the fringe of a culture contributes an observation that isn't a tool for solving a problem in either her culture or the beneficiary's culture, it isn't wisdom so much as it is the beginning of shift paradigms in different segments of society. It is an insight that allows dialogue and education that may change a way of life for the world. If nothing else, the observation makes clear the predicament that a way of life faces.

Michel Foucault's "empirical orders prescribed for [a culture] by its primary code" encompasses what is referred to as wisdom that various populations follow to solve problems. (xxii) These populations may be local or groups within larger groups. In this case, I refer to youth culture (via popular music) and middle-brow or high artistic cultures (that are outside or more complicated than youth culture) within a culture defined by language and hemisphere. I also refer to a culture from outside the language / hemispheric culture as one that brings a greater and liberating insight.

Therefore, youth culture would then possess wisdom, artistic cultures would possess cultural wisdom and perhaps attempt transcendence, and outside cultures (with different language and global location) may possess insight from that vantage point.

In this essay, I illustrate a progression from folk wisdom to cultural wisdom to outsider insight. The cultural wisdom is at least idealized as transcending a cultural tradition and may be seen as an attempt to break empirical orders of primary codes. I also hope to shed light on an insight that perhaps only a novice or outside observer of a particular tradition may offer. I would not refer to the contribution as wisdom. I am contending in this essay that Mick Jagger's folk wisdom in his lyrics to "As Tears Go By," resembles lines in W. B. Yeats' more universal Western ideal "Sailing to Byzantium." Though Yeats' poem is more ambitious than the song lyrics by attempting to escape place and time, it does return to the roots of the wisdom or empirical order of a primary code because it returns to the historical roots of the tradition. Yeats' is a cultural wisdom. Even more ambitious is Gayatri Chakravorty Spivak's insight from a cultural margin or outside the culture altogether in her essay "Reading the World." Spivak sheds light on both genres using a similar thought but naming the primary code as a naked emperor.

Considering the three expressions that point out repetition in culture, Spivak's is the most consequential. Where Jagger's is folk wisdom and Yeats' is an attempt transcendental wisdom, Spivak is cultural and political insight. Once the population becomes conscious about the repetition it has been involved in it makes sense that that population would ask why the repetition and whether it is necessary. For Jagger's "As Tears Go By" and Yeats' "Sailing to Byzantium" the repetition is the generation of people through time. Spivak, in "Reading the World," suggests that the technological and capitalistic repetition through the generations is one of winners and losers where even masters may also be slaves. The questions why and necessary are packed with significance. We are set on a horizon and challenged to stop playing the same old song.

To explain differing vantage points of a greater culture by people who are inside, those attempting to escape, and outside, or others on the fringe of the culture, one might refer to cultures as spheres of influence. I am interested in what Foucault's cultural paradigm and the degrees that those empirical orders (wisdom included) are set or breached by cultural leaders or newcomers: lyricists, poets, and cultural critics. Within the cultural sphere, people go about what has been called nature's trick, the rage of hormones cloaked in romance or other courting rituals and then the rituals around death: generations' life cycles. I don't believe that the cultural spheres mentioned in the essay are analogous to the Plato's cave because first I am attempting to explain not reality as an abstract but something peculiar to cultures. If the culture were to be perceived as a cave, then there would be many caves and the inhabitants of various caves would then bring insights to other caves, a kind of cross pollination of empirical orders.

Here and there around the greater cultural sphere are the spokes-persons or cultural leaders who report on the goings on within the culture sometimes with local insight and wisdom regarding the culture's peoples' situation, the fornication and last breaths, or about the relationship between the spokesperson and the people in the sphere of influence. The reporting is to those people within that particular culture. Often the reporting by the spokesperson is done through music that the culture enjoys. The spokespersons may even make the information seem new. The report through music might be called folk music though today it is often called popular music or rock-'n-roll. But because it is reporting on the generations within the sphere of influence, it is folk music for a specific generation and each generation lays claim to its own, "the golden oldies" of any generation. The folk spokesperson confirms the culture's empirical order and primary code. Great solace is taken hearing the music and lyrics again and again as folk wisdom.

Sometimes the spokesperson learns something strange from another culture or from a different time, new information about outside the sphere of influence. The experience is frightening and threatening to the spokesperson. Sometimes the spokesperson may be attempting to break out of the empirical order of the primary code, a truly awesome feat even at its daring. These spokespersons, perhaps artists, attempt to put distance, between themselves and what may be considered folk or wisdom or parochial for something grander and perhaps more vital to the culture. Sometimes a spokesperson may refer to their offering as universal. They may view the folk within the culture including those with folk wisdom as mortal constituents. These spokespersons for the greater culture reveal themselves sometimes as elitists. The artists may reveal to the folk inside the sphere of influence what is perceived to be outside of the cultural symbols and perhaps tell of a world of cultures. These spokespersons are artists and poets, and they attempt to breach the sphere of influence of folk culture and the greater culture in an attempt to bring new information about outside the greater culture (or to "climb out" of time and space) believing that their work might be relevant for a longer period of time than a generation.

As the reporters for the outside and inside of the culture, the spokespersons entertain and distract each generation of folk, hoping to at least remind but perhaps enlighten the literate folk and sphere of influence officials. The description of the internal and external nature of the familiar cultures, vital to the artists and poets, is what differentiates them from the folk inside the familiar cultures, the lyricists, and the more literate populations. The kind of wisdom reported may be confirmation of a culture's primary code or it may breach the empirical order and propose a new empirical order or new primary code. In any case, the reporting is their contribution to the greater cultural conversation, to a "final vocabulary" of sorts in a more significant way than the reporting by the folk spokes-person lyricist.

Again, staying with the idea of the greater culture, there is another person who is perhaps from another sphere of influence, another greater culture, and may even be the kind of person not usually respected by folks inside original culture or the artists of that culture. This person, also a reporter, is not a spokesperson but perhaps would be best described as a person contributing insight to the original culture from another culture. This reporter may be seen as a novice and may bring a fresh way of seeing things or perhaps recognizing the obvious that is either unspoken or taboo and speaking it. This person reports the relevance of the insight to the folks within the original sphere of influence and names the contents and maker of the unspoken, an act that if made conscious to the population would threaten the whole greater culture with a paradigm shift.

Concentric spheres of influence may help explain the relationship among Mick Jagger's lyrics to "As Tears Go By," W.B. Yeats's "Sailing to Byzantium," and in her essay "Reading the World," Gayatri Chakravorty Spivak's concept of the West as "disc jockey of an advanced technocracy:" "the most recent technology" as a means of denying freedom by distracting populations. By situating the three different kinds of reporters, folk artist Jagger, high modernist poet Yeats, and postcolonial/critical theorist Spivak I am trying to bring a little more clarity about the relationships among these three reporters or spokespersons.

Recently, Martin Scorsese filmed The Rolling Stones on tour. With the group's members in their sixties, it may be their last tour. When Jagger was a young man he wrote and sang "As Tears Go By" before handing it off to Maryanne Faithful. Mick sang it on the tour and in the film. His aging brittle voice was very affective with the song, seeming to bring the power of wisdom to it. Indeed the years had gone by and that underscored the lyrics. In the song we find the lines, "Doin' things I used to do they think are new. / I sit and watch as tears go by." Jagger's persona in this lyric is not staccato but jolting, tough, and now lacking fluidity. The word "tears" is a pun for years and its accumulation of tears. Jagger is distinguishing young from old, drawing a romantic line of winners and losers. The losers are the old, wise ones who recognize each loss as a tear drop. The lyrics may be said to celebrate the wisdom of folk in the form of insight or a reminder of the primary code that the culture belongs to the young.

The lyric may also be seen as a commentary on the music world itself. The persona may be pointing out that young musicians believe that they are carving out new territory much the way he thought he was, only to find later that it isn't new ground at all. The music seems new to the uneducated ear whose lips whistle or sing the tunes while at work or play and allow the musician to make a living performing the songs. Understood in this way, a musician might ask: what is one to do in a world where nothing is new or original? How does a pop musician breech the empirical order of the primary code? How does a musician insure an audience after his/her death? In Jagger's case he continues to sing and louder sing and hopes for the best, perhaps capturing a particular mood for a generation. However, he has lived a very comfortable life as a reporter for folk culture, one that his fans envy. He does thank the crowd and tell them that he loves them in the Scorcese film.

**As Tears Go By**

It is the evening of the day,
I sit and watch the children play.
Smiling faces I can see, but not for me,
I sit and watch as tears go by.

My riches can't buy ev'rything,
I want to hear the children sing.

All I hear is the sound of rain falling on the ground,
I sit and watch as tears go by.

It is the evening of the day,
I sit and watch the children play.
Doin' things I used to do they think are new.
I sit and watch as tears go by.

The lyric is similar to Yeats' "In one another's arms, birds in the trees /- Those dying generations - at their song," yet Yeats reverses the winners and losers by having the poet "Sailing to Byzantium" as the winner surviving the "salmon-falls" and "paltry" things as a Grecian goldsmith. It goes further by drawing a line between the citizens seduced by nature's trick to provide another generation of citizenry and the poet whose words keep emperors awake. Both lyric and poem distinguish between the wisdom of older persona and the naïve young citizens. (191) While one may argue that the persona of the song lyric values the position of the child over his position as purveyor of wisdom, the reader of the poem can only sense the desperation of a persona attempting immortality via Harold Bloom's "strong poet" concept. Here the persona may be said to be not only poking through the but attempting to run away from the circus by reporting on an older tent city and longer lasting wisdom than the tent pole lyric crafter has to offer, a more reliable cultural tool.

### Sailing To Byzantium

That is no country for old men. The young
In one another's arms, birds in the trees
- Those dying generations - at their song,
The salmon-falls, the mackerel-crowded seas,
Fish, flesh, or fowl, commend all summer long
Whatever is begotten, born, and dies.
Caught in that sensual music all neglect
Monuments of unageing intellect.

An aged man is but a paltry thing,
A tattered coat upon a stick, unless
Soul clap its hands and sing, and louder sing
For every tatter in its mortal dress,
Nor is there singing school but studying
Monuments of its own magnificence;
And therefore I have sailed the seas and come
To the holy city of Byzantium.

O sages standing in God's holy fire
As in the gold mosaic of a wall,

> Come from the holy fire, perne in a gyre,
> And be the singing-masters of my soul.
> Consume my heart away; sick with desire
> And fastened to a dying animal
> It knows not what it is; and gather me
> Into the artifice of eternity.
>
> Once out of nature I shall never take
> My bodily form from any natural thing,
> But such a form as Grecian goldsmiths make
> Of hammered gold and gold enamelling
> To keep a drowsy Emperor awake;
> Or set upon a golden bough to sing
> To lords and ladies of Byzantium
> Of what is past, or passing, or to come. (191)

A similar idea as each of the above lyrics and poem can be found in a passage by Gayatri Chakravorty Spivak. It must be admitted that she was a biographer and scholar of W. B. Yeats early in her career. Her passage complicates the above ideas. In her book *In Other Worlds*, Gayatri Chakravorty Spivak wrote,

> We are the disc jockeys of an advanced technology. The discs are not "records" of the old fashioned kind, but productions of the most recent technology. The trends in taste and the economic factors that govern them are also products of the most complex interrelations among a myriad of factors as foreign relations, the world market, the conduct of advertisement supported by and supporting the first two items, and so on…Within his intricately determined and multiform situation, the disc jockey and his audience think, indeed are made to think, that they are free to play. This illusion of freedom allows us to protect the brutal ironies of technocracy by suggesting either that the system nourishes the humanist's freedom of spirit, or that "technology," that vague evil, is something the humanist must transform by inculcating humanistic "values," or by drawing generalized philosophical analogies from the latest spatio-temporal discoveries of the magical realms of "pure science." (128-129)

In her prose, Spivak suggests that the capitalism's slave-citizens are generations of children doing things they think are new. The earlier song lyric is folk wisdom charged with insight or reminder of the primary code; the poem is an argument for cultural wisdom by a member of that culture attempting to breech empirical order with an universal transcendence; and the essay is an explanation of the collusion of science, technology, and capitalism presented as postcolonial and critical insight from someone who might be said to be outside the culture, outside the lyricist's and poet's sphere of influence. Perhaps she is someone with badly needed critical or radical insight that may seem a clarion call to the folk but who is in reality announcing a need for a paradigm shift.

One could argue as to which is more intricate thinking, but Jagger's would always come out the loser. Of course, he wasn't trying to do anything more than present folk wisdom, reminding a generation of the empirical order. Spivak's meta-insight is most powerful for its complexity and simplicity. What the three representations illustrate to the reader is the telescopic insight first between the subaltern and exploiter of emotions; then the insight of a literate time-traveler that poses as profound rationalization for the traveler's sense of what roots the culture's empirical order; and finally what Jean-Francois Lyotard would call a differend or here an outsider as a novice or child who might proclaim that the emperor lacks clothing.

Spivak who, is Indian, does not make a saw from a hammer in her analysis. What she may be doing first is pointing out the process for making a hammer a saw. However, more importantly her articulation of a process that isn't the manufacturing of quaint cultural wisdom into a more universal tool as it is a global insight regarding an economic system (becoming more and more universal) perpetuating an illusion to keep the children playing, the generations at their song, the adult worker enslaved. Her insight isn't wisdom because it isn't problem-solving but problem-posing. She brings a consciousness from outside a culture. The idea of the same song using different technology is different from "generations at their song" or "children doing things I use to do" in that it points out a laboratory to the white rats in it, not a trick of nature but a man-made artifice. Making conscious the problem of a techno-capitalism as something other than creative play, "a vague evil," Spivak makes conscious that the latest spatio-temporal discoveries are the magical realms of "pure science." The more lab rats educated to the thought that they are slaves, the more they want freedom from the lab.

After reading theorists, it is difficult for a poet to go back to writing the poems that a poet was writing earlier in his/her career if he/she had only read other poets and listened to popular music, no matter what they were. His/her thinking ignores empirical orders and primary codes or as Foucault might have said arrived at the "middle region which liberates order itself." (xxi) The poet is no longer satisfied with the limited reading of many other poets but satisfied only when reading broadly also and then contemplating the various ideas in light of his/her particular concrete culture and art, folk or cosmopolitan in nature.

Does one reply to the thinkers? Where does a poet go from where his/her culture is? How does a poet acknowledge globalization and its cross-pollination and respect the individual spheres that harbor cultures, even with their pernicious natures? These are the questions that a contemporary poet needs to ponder or risk playing into the hands of a culture's propaganda and its powerful forces. Certainly poets have always read widely as they read their poetic traditions. After all, the poet learns as much from the philosopher as the philosopher from the poet: Practice and theory. Today, poetic justice needs to be running round-the-clock sessions in its higher courts.

## WORKS CITED

Foucault, Michel. *The Order of Things*. New York: Random House, 1970.
Jagger, Mick. "As Tears Go By." Performance in *Shine a Light*, a documentary film by Martin Scorcese. Paramount, 2008.
Spivak, Gayatri Chakravorty. "Reading the World: Literary Studies in the Eighties." *In Other Worlds*, New York: Routledge, 1998, pp. 128-29.
Yeats, William Butler. "Sailing to Byzantium." *The Collected Poems of W. B. Yeats*, New York: MacMillan, 1974, p.191.

CHAPTER 3

## Spectacle and Aporia in Ted Kooser and John Ashbery

Beauty is a blind alley. It is a mountain peak which once reached leads nowhere. That is why in the end we find more to entrance in El Greco than in Titian, in the incomplete achievement of Shakespeare than in the consummate success of Racine. Too much has been written about beauty. That is why I have written a little more. Beauty is that which satisfies the aesthetic instinct. But who wants to be satisfied? It is only the dullard that enough is as good as a feast. Let us face it: beauty is a bit of a bore.
(W. Somerset Maugham, 1930)

The question of postmodernism is also, or first of all, a question of expressions of thought: in art, literature, philosophy, and politics ... a kind of work, a long obstinate, and highly responsible work concerned with investigating the assumptions implicit in modernity.
(Jean-Francois Lyotard, 1984)

In his book *Mythologies,* Roland Barthes' first chapter "The World of Wrestling" analyzes the "grandiloquence" of the spectacle of the so-called sport and finds in it that of the ancient theatre and Greek drama. Barthes celebrates wrestling because he sees that in its grandiloquence is the morality passion play of ancient Greece. In the chapter, he tells us that the sport is "the spectacle of excess" (15). He finds in its grandiloquence the same "as that of the ancient theatre, whose principle, language and props (masks and buskins) concurred in the exaggeratedly visible explanation of a Necessity" (16). Later he continues,

> There is no more a problem of truth in wrestling than in the theatre. In both, what is expected is the intelligible representation of moral situations which are usually private. The emptying out of the interiority to the benefit of its exterior signs, this exhaustion of the content by the form, is the very principle of triumphant classical art. (18)

In finding the structure of wrestling to be that of ancient theatre in general and ancient Greek drama in particular, Barthes is recognizing what James Joyce recognized when he wrote *Ulysses*. Joyce noticed that recognizable patterns and harmonies in literature satisfy the audience and make legitimate the symbols of the day, suggesting that they indeed do hold something. However, where Joyce seems to be making critical commentary on his day with his anti-hero de-legitimizing his society's behavior and re-legitimizing ancient Greek drama, Barthes is legitimizing contemporary activities as dramatic, religious rituals as worthy as Greek literature. He is finding the beauty that lies in the spectacle of excess in popular culture. Joyce holds the present up to the mythological past for comparison in order to make it new. Barthes suggests spectacle can't be made new. In fact, he sees that beauty is a meta-narrative for the spectacle of excess.

The reader comes away with the idea that using the "spectacle of excess" as a lens he/she may examine other events in our society and find the beauty of Greek drama. The reader also comes away with the notion that spectacle of excess may be modernity's beauty. One can observe it most easily in staged events that are meant to attract the masses to witness "Suffering, Defeat, and Justice" played out (19). Examples of it can be found on reality television and staged programming such as sitcoms as well. Barthes suggests that beauty is the emptying out of symbolic form inherent in the spectacle of excess to the satisfaction of the audience. If one looks closely at poetic works in modernism, one can see that the poets are performing that function. Just as we find in popular culture's staged events, we find the spectacle of excess possesses beauty in poetry. Poetry that resolves irony with the justice of closure is using beauty to articulate its experience. Beauty might be said to be the intelligible representation of moral situations that are often private and that are emptied out of their interiority to the benefit of its exterior signs and the audience (18).

It is the satisfaction of justice witnessed that one finds in the spectacle and in the legitimating power of its performance of morality that is also known as beauty. The satisfaction of harmony, symmetry, and the promise and performance of oneness to audiences / "spectators" builds society and culture with its shared experience. This same satisfaction found in recognizing ourselves in a storyline or a scene in a play or an image in a poem is the joy of recognizing the language game as familiar and safe. We know the game and if that isn't enough we are witnesses of the situation in the literature after all. We are present metaphorically.

Throughout modern poetry we find great beauty in its spectacle of excess in every line, of every sentence. The poem starts with the promise that needs performing. The performing is the emptying of the symbols. The emptying is one of alliteration, allusion, simile, contemporary images, and other devices of harmony that reassure the audience of purging of symbol that is taking place. Even if the images are ugly, if they are familiar they satisfy the reader.

However, there is always a place where the poet in his/her attempts to give the spectators / audience the emotional experience of the plot or event beyond language. When the author attempts to inspire and to possess words with a kind of madness and divine spirit as Longinus might suggest, the author "'carries the hearer along with the [sublime] involuntarily'" with "'a kind of violence rather than by cool conviction'" (Shaw 14). Kant clarifies the sublime as something not in nature by telling us that the sublime is contained in our minds. Derrida is summarized on the secular postmodern sublime: "The experience and pleasure of the sublime do not stem from the promise of something noumenal, outside a given frame, but rather the perpetual, yet always provisional, activity of framing itself, from the *parergon*" (Shaw 118). The spectacle of beauty sets up the audience for the sublime moment. Beauty frames sublime as modern poetry. By "set up" I mean allowing the reader to trust the writer for three-quarters of the way through a text with familiar representational conventions until the writer confronts the reader with the idea that the only conventions we have are the ones we make, driving the poem's point home. Modern poetry may or may not have the Romantic's transcendental sublime. However, it is most often of the Longinus variety of sublime of inexplicable passion.

If we recognize the non-transcendental sublime or aporia, we find that we are "without way or passage," at an abyss, something open and unresolved that inspires doubt and "difficulty in choosing" (Royle 92). We have something more threatening than beauty. In his book *Aporias,* Derrida defines it as,

> a matter of the nonpassage, or rather from the experience of the nonpassage, the experience of what happens and is fascinating in this nonpassage, paralyzing in this separation in a way that is not necessarily negative: before a door, threshold, border, a line, or simply the edge or the approach of the other as such. It should be a matter of what, in sum, appears to block our way or to separate us in the very place where it would no longer be possible to constitute a problem, a project, or a projection, that is, at the point where the very project or the problematic task becomes impossible and where we are exposed, absolutely without protection, without problem, and without prosthesis, without possible substitution, singularly exposed in our absolute and absolutely naked uniqueness, that is to say disarmed, delivered to the other, incapable even of sheltering ourselves behind what could still protect the interiority of a secret. (12)

Aporia is a concern for all frames, a reminder that there are no frames except for the ones we make. The poem is not going to lead the reader to a sublime moment but challenge the frames of the familiar, the beautiful, the harmony at every turn of phrase. So when the familiar or conventional performs as a frame or parergon, aporia emerges. The frame promises convention while aporia disturbs as the nonpassage. However, it isn't a transcendental sublime. There isn't an imitation of a higher power. Perhaps Jean-Francois Lyotard explains the Postmodern sublime aporia best when he says, "'Presenting the existence of something unpresentable. Showing that there is something we can conceive of that we can neither see nor show'" (29). In Simon Malpas' book *The Postmodern*, he summarizes Lyotard:

> The postmodern artist or writer is in the position of a philosopher: the text he writes or the work he creates is not in principle governed by preestablished rules and cannot be judged...by the application of given categories to this text or work. Such rules and categories are what the work or text is investigating. (30)

The difference between modern poetry and postmodern poetry can be attributed to modern poetry's putting forward the sublime as "missing contents," and postmodern poetry as ignoring beauty and form to attempt to put forward the unpresentable. In

*Prophetic Voice Now*

fact Lyotard sees the relationship between modern and postmodern not as historical moments but as styles, shifting back and forth. Modern art first may be Postmodern until it is familiar or conventional and then it is Modern. With Barthes' idea of spectacle and Derrida's sublime aporia as lenses, this paper argues that when poetry becomes modern and familiar, it becomes a thing of beauty, a spectacle of excess. When it is postmodern, it is a spectacle of the sublime.

The poetry of Ted Kooser and John Ashbery bears this out. Kooser is the most popular poet in the USA and has recently been its Poet Laureate. Ashbery is said to be the most important poet writing in English today. However, Ashbery's work is unknown or inaccessible to most of the population in the USA. How does one explain this apparent paradox? One may reply that one is modern, and one is postmodern. One writes beautiful poetry or poetry that embraces the spectacle of excess and attempts the sublime at some point in each poem. The other writes poetry employing sublime aporia as its instrumental tool. One writes using pre-established rules, and one does not, as Lyotard explains. But a closer look at the two poets' work may be more revealing.

In Ted Kooser's Pulitzer Prize winning book, *Shadows and Delights*, any of the poems would serve as an example of modern poetry using my definition. "Tattoo," the short second poem in the collection, is a poem beautiful in its spectacle and will serve my purposes in this short paper. (6) "Tattoo" is modern in that Kooser is not looking for dignity in his choice of subject but revealing the subject's dignity to the reader. It is modern also because readers expect the revealing, the emptying of the poetry. Any subject is fair game. The images he brings that include a thug grown old are familiar to Americans: a yard sale, a shoulder with a tattoo, a schoolyard bully. What is new in this poem is not the images. There are harmonies in his walking between the tables, the bruise gone "soft and blue," and youthful vanity gone bony with age's self-recognition and yet insisting on what was once (6). Even the abused broken tools as fragments of the bully's youth or stories of that youth are familiar and are a spectacle of excess. It is a great poem of a defeated middle-class suburbanite persona finding justice.

**Tattoo**

What once was meant to be a statement—
a dripping dagger held in the fist
of a shuddering heart—is now just a bruise
on a bony old shoulder, the spot
where vanity once punched him hard
and the ache lingered on. He looks like
someone you had to reckon with,
strong as a stallion, fast and ornery,
but on this chilly morning, as he walks
between the tables at a yard sale
with the sleeves of his tight black T-shirt
rolled up to show us who he was,

> he is only another old man, picking up
> broken tools and putting them back,
> his heart gone soft and blue with stories.

The reader knows this story of withering powers and regret brought on by growing old and so anticipates "[t]he emptying out of the interiority to the benefit of its exterior signs" (Barthes 18). Kooser heightens the story by using the familiar motorcycle culture imagery and flattens the magnified image that the bullied persona has of the predator using the yard sale and the line "only another old man" (6). The satisfaction that the reader receives from the execution of this poem is the same as Barthes reveals in wrestling spectacles. It is the execution of justice, a kind of justice that Nietzsche attributes to slaves and Christians, a justice long after the crimes were committed, a kind of no justice that is not witnessed except in the minds of the victims. The language and props…concur in exaggeratedly visible explanation and description (Barthes 16).

What Kooser may be making new in the "make it new" sense of modernism is the familiar, common everyday world. He also may be making new the poem's subject, the persona and not the biker. The poem may be read as the persona and the other old man as one person, using the conventional double. The persona is not a witness recording the events a la Confessional School but the poet as tough guy gone "blue with stories" (6). The first line introduces the reader to "a statement" of youth and then reveals what the symbol tattoos in every poem of the youthful male poet: one of masculine passion and virility. A reader unschooled might contend that Kooser's poem is an attempt to "show us who he was." The broken tools are his apology to the reader for the fragments that he is shoring against his ruin.

In fact, Kooser attempts to nudge the reader to consider the sublime is in his line, "rolled up to show us who he was" (6). On one level the reader is expecting "who he is" because the sleeves are rolled up and he dresses as in his youth but bringing in the past tense throws the justice-seeking reader off the end of the line with satisfaction while the line points at the terror of the inevitable powerlessness of old age. Here he is also humbly offering to the reader the fragments of his former virility as a poet. Read on either level, the persona is performing the same "necessity" as Barthes' wrestlers whether the reader understands the poem to be about the bully of bike culture or the life of a poet.

In John Ashbery's *As We Know,* the title poem is a good example of his developed style and typical of the shorter poems in the book. Where Kooser meets the reader with the beauty of familiar images and leads the reader to the moment of the sublime that is the subject, Ashbery's poems are inaccessible to most readers to this day and this poem is no exception. However, once the reader recognizes that Ashbery is not meeting the reader on the reader's terms but reminding the reader with each sentence that language itself can merely point or gesture at the poet's subject, the reader has a chance to come to grips with his poetry. The busy reader going about the day "making a living" and pretending that, and taking for granted that what is before him is knowable, thanks Kooser for coming into the reader's world of pretense and escorting sensibility to Longinus' insight. Busy readers are confronted with aporias that make up an Ashbery poem. In fact the title itself takes a common notion and turns it on its head. The confidence of the common platitude becomes a meditation on the fleeting nature of knowing.

**As We Know**

All that we see is penetrated by it—
The distant treetops with their steeple (so
Innocent), the stair, the windows' fixed flashing—
Pierced full of holes by the evil that is not evil,
The romance that is not mysterious, the life that is not life,
A present that is elsewhere.

And further in the small capitulations
Of the dance, you rub elbows with it,
Finger it. That day you did it
Was the day you had to stop, because the doing
Involved the whole fabric, there was no other way to appear.
You slid down on your knees
For those precious jewels of spring water
Planted on the moss, before they got soaked up
And you teetered on the edge of this
Calm street with its sidewalks, its traffic,

As though they are coming to you.
But there was on one in the noon glare,
Only birds like secrets to find out about
And home to get to, one of these days.

The light that was shadowed then
Was seen to be our lives.
Everything about us that love might wish to examine,

Then put away for a certain length of time, until
The whole is to be reviewed, and we turned
Toward each other, to each other.
The way we had come was all we could see
And it crept up on us, embarrassed
That there is so much to tell now, really now.

The first sentence / section of "As We Know" is an example. In the first line, "All that we see is penetrated by it--" what does Ashbery mean by "it:" light, evil that is not evil, life that is not live, air (74)? Any of these will do for now. We can see light moving through the trees surrounding a steeple, innocent because of human declaration only and the windows flashing, glaring as well as the metal lining that prevents leaks. But what is described as an "evil that is not evil...life that is not life" adds intricacy but does not necessarily block or shade the penetration that is splashed at the reader's feet: "A present that is elsewhere" (74). The reader has little chance at getting familiar with any image because the images that he gives the reader are fragmented. The reader must see the poem's imagery as a part of the process that is the experience of experience, the poet insisting the experience of the poem's now. The giving and taking away that he does in this first sentence itself and through it is aporia, the nontranscendental sublime of Derrida: the fascinating, paralyzing, not necessarily negative experience of the nonpassage (12). The first lines permeate with the unpresentable now of a Barnett Newman painting. It also demonstrates through lines 2-5 the penetration of a present that is not, at least any longer. The permeation theme calls to mind Burroughs' *Naked Lunch*.

The second section invests the reader in a drama without the "we" of the first. The drama or "dance" is the anticipation of the now. During the dance of life we merely rub elbows with the present, perhaps "finger it," but trying to wear it, one has to stop because it is impossible to appear the way one appears already by living in the present (74). The most one can do is get on one's knees and soak up the precious jewels of the moment. The drama spills over into the third passage where it becomes the regret and fear of a past now. As close as we get to capturing the moment passing is our teetering on the "edge of this / Calm street" (74). Throughout the building of the reader's investment in the second passage, aporia reigns. "[T]he small capitulations / Of the dance," is a case in point. The negative of capitulation is undercut by the dance (and vice versa), keeping the reader in the present tense of "finger it" (74).

The third section reminds this reader of the existential Lowell lines "nobody's here--/ only skunks" in "Skunk Hour" (95). The anxiety of Ashbery's first section is denied by the second line: "no one in the noon glare, / Only birds" (74). Unlike Lowell though, Ashbery presents aporia in the first two lines and in the "secrets to find out about," where we recognize that we don't recognize (74). The home the reader is urged toward is not made of wood or brick or stone. It is the reader's demise.

The last section picks up on death with the idea of the shadows of lives and again includes the voice along with the reader: "Everything about us" (74). Here the voice suggests that the reader, the voice, and everything is shadowed (or is shadow) so that love's examination of the reader and voice is not possible. The nuance of the lines "and we turned / Toward each other, to each other" reminds the reader of the relationship of the poet and the reader, and that even this confrontation of love on the page cannot capture the magnitude of now's so much to tell (74). The light and shadow as lives, love examining, the gathering of experience, our way that crept on us, and the embarrassment of experience's stories are all examples of aporia in this poem. Over and over the poem demonstrates to the reader the fragmented process of consciousness, the rung by rung climb up Wittgenstein's ladder resulting in this poem.

What David Shapiro in his essay "The Mirror Staged" refers to as "*deferred sense*" or "meaning absenting itself" in Ashbery's poetry is what Derrida means by aporia. Where we may find aporia at the height of a modernist poem is where the poet attempts to go beyond words to bring the passion of his/her meaning to the reader.

Postmodern poetry distorts in order to rescue the value of distortion (5). In the distortion is the poem tracing the mind tracing a poem (11). Postmodern poetry attempts aporia in every sentence if not in the fragmentation of imagery; unresolved irony is key. In every "denial of intrinsic *logos*" the reader is confronted with the postmodern sublime (30). These qualities in postmodern poetry are confrontational in a culture that survives on sound bites, platitudes, clichés, and jingles. The pretense of communication demands that its participants be reminded of the pretense. Line after line, sentence after sentence of rescuers of distortion's value is aporia reminding the reader of possibility, other realities waiting for them. The poet's job then becomes one of merely suggesting a statement through the poet's variations on themes, promoting a healthy respect for the gap between the signified and signifier.

Ashbery's poem "Litany" is in the same collection of poems. Too long to examine in this paper, however, the 65-page poem is made up two columns "to be read as two simultaneous but independent monologues" (2). What kind of trick is this? This kind: the poem itself is aporia, extended parallel tracts that don't meet. In the first 31 lines of the first column ending in "Code names for silence" and the first 26 lines of the second column ending in "About to happen" we can see subtly opposing or better yet isolated voices: one embracing the past and the other embracing a fantasy future (4).

For someone like me
The simple things
Like having toast or
Going to church are
Kept in one place.

Like having wine and cheese.

The parents of the town
Pissing elegantly escape knowledge
Once and for all. The
Snapdragons consumed in the wind
Of fire and rage far over
The streets as they end.

The casual purring of a donkey
Rouses me from my accounts:
What given, what gifts. The air
Stands straight up like a tail.

He spat on the flowers.

Also for someone
Like me the time flows round again
With things I did in it.
I wish to keep my differences

And to retain my kinship
To the rest. That is why
I raise these flowers all around.
They do not stand for flowers or
Anything pretty they are
Code names for the silence.

So this must be a hole
Of cloud
Mandate or trap
But haze that casts
The milk of enchantment

Over the whole town,
Its scenery, whatever
Could be happening
Behind tall hedges
Of dark, lissome knowledge.

The brown lines persist
In explicit sex
Matters like these
No one can care about,
"Noone." That is I've said it
Before and no one
Remembers except that elf.

Around us are signposts
Pointing to the past,
The old-fashioned, pointed
Wooden kind. And nothing directs
To the present that is

About to happen.

The voice of column one is infatuated with the assurance of one concrete place perhaps being served wine and cheese at a reception would provide, and with the stillness of dead streets and "air standing straight up like a tail" of a donkey, a stubborn animal whose breathing complaint spits on flowers. In an effort to escape knowledge of reality, the voice is one living in the past, with time flowing around it again containing things it did (3). The voice raises silence around it as though silence were flowers or anything pretty and reaffirming.

In the second column, the voice is no place, a cloud that is a trap or "milk of enchantment" (3). As the pissing "Parents of the town" in the first column "escape knowledge" by living in the past, the concrete place here is the scenery "behind hedges of dark lissome knowledge" (3). Matters of explicit sex that "No one can care about" are not acknowledged by people (3). Avoiding knowledge seems to be the only thing these two voices have in common. Only an elf remembers everything in the second column. As the flowers are codes of silence in the first column, signposts point to the past in the second where nothing directs "to the present that is" and is "about to happen" (4) As one voice lives in the silence of the past, the other lives in fantasy, the place of the future. Neither is attempting to live in the present, perhaps an impossible but perhaps worthy task. The aporetic gap exists between the two approaches that the two voices use to live life: through the past and through fantasy. Ashbery is commenting on the fleeting nature of the present. If the poem is read as critical commentary on the postmodern world we live in, it is because the voices in the poem flee from notions of the present, fearing perhaps their impotence regarding it. Neither voice recognizes the possibility of the sublime moment of now.

Modern poetry through representation makes new the subject matter of its poetry. The transformation of the subject matter is an attempt at therapy for the writer and reader, an attempt to reveal the beauty and sublime in what might be construed as ugly: Pound's imagist poem "In a Station at the Metro," for example. Substitute Barthes' spectacle of excess for beauty, and it makes new representation in Kooser's poetry as it does in modern poetry. Through the excess emerges the sublime moment of the poem.

Postmodernism interrogates representation, and using aporias confronts attempts at therapy with a relentless barrage of possibility at a foundational level of language. So Ashbery's poetry is a spectacle in its public display and an excess of a different kind. Nothing physical is being represented. Ashbery's excess is the relentless line by line attempt at the unpresentable. The relentless aporias are reminders of the possible worlds contemporary society refuses to inhabit.

If the world of modern poetry uses the spectacle of excess as beauty for therapeutic purposes, then it is where it was in Tennyson's day, or worse it is a reassurance that all is right with the world that capitalism controls. If so, poetry substitutes for a snooze or a venture to a flea market on a Sunday afternoon. Modern poetry gets lost in its compromise with the reader and beauty. Modern poetry may indeed save lives one at a time. However, postmodern poetry calls for among other things last ditch gestures. It challenges the concept of making it new with exhilarating meditations on the possible worlds that are being lost in each moment of the now

## WORKS CITED

Ashbery, John. *As We Know*. New York: Penguin Books, 1979.
Barthes, Roland. *Mythologies*. Translated by Annette Lavers. New York: Hill and Wang, 1972.
Derrida, Jacques. *Aporias*. Translated by Thomas Dutoit. Stanford: Stanford University Press, 1993.
Kooser, Ted. *Delights & Shadows*. Port Townsend: Copper Canyon Press, 2004.
Lowell, Robert. *The Selected Poems*. New York: Farrar, Straus, and Giroux, 1977.
Lyotard, Jean-Francois. *The Sublime*. Ed. Philip Shaw. New York: Routledge, 2006.
Malpas, Simon. *The Postmodern*. New York: Routledge, 2005.
Royle, Nicholas. *Jacques Derrida*. New York: Routledge, 2003.
Shapiro, David. *John Ashbery: An Introduction to the Poetry*. New York: Columbia University Press, 1979.

CHAPTER 4

## The Hopkins Path to Postmodern Poetry

In his essay "The Figure a Poem Makes," Robert Frost defines poetry as "a momentary stay against confusion," (2008, http://www.mrbauld.com/frostfig.html) Frost's phrase may be one of his most quoted contributions to poetics. Frost may have been suggesting that with scientific and technological progress or Enlightenment thinking changing things so quickly and grandly that momentary pauses were all that a culture had to offer and suggesting also that poetry and art needed to be unifiers producing those pauses or stays against confusion. If art were a unifier, the arts took on a very large responsibility. Art attempted to hold onto religion and science, tradition and reason. Art then mourned the loss of religion and tradition. Finally, it celebrated humans free and responsible, free and responsible without religion, tradition, and reason. Literary canons could not hold and a technological anarchy was loosed upon the world, the world that we learn finds its origins in cosmic catastrophe.

I would like to propose that there have been three attitudes that poetry has projected during three consecutive eras since the Enlightenment in the West. The first is one of desperation caused by the threat of science and commerce in the Victorian era. The second is a sense of mourning and longing for unity in modernity that religion and tradition provided. The third attitude is one of celebration of freedom from the past, tempered by responsibility that can be found in the postmodern arts, a freedom from tradition that religion provided and enforced. Gerard Manley Hopkins is more than representative of the first era. In his desperation, he discovers the foundation for the poetry of the modern and postmodern poet. The idea within inscape that changes as the attitude of each age changes is instress. The definition of instress changes for poets as science and technology more and more replace religious tradition. It changes further as the responsibility and freedom that postmodernism implies seeps into a culture devoid of art.

What makes an unknown poet develop while remaining religiously enthusiastic enough to become a convert to Catholicism? (If being an unknown poet and convert isn't a desperate situation, then using poetry to demonstrate conversion certainly is.) If we keep in mind that the Victorian age was one of a return to orthodoxy in the face of the rising threat of the bourgeois materialism and Enlightenment's physicality, we might understand the pull of religious order to an unknown poet. Darwinian science threatened traditional thought: Evolution denied the bible's accounts of the creation of humans and challenged religious morality. Darwin's theory also showed that humans were a part of nature and assumed that there wasn't a purposeful God. Holding tradition together must have been very superficial while science was threatening religious thought and challenging the hierarchical way of life with its technological promise to the middle class.

In *Dragon in the Gate*, (1969) Elisabeth Schneider's account of "The Wreck of the Deutschland" may help us understand Hopkins' situation. Earlier in her book she reminds us that Hopkins's conversion and his entrance into a Jesuit order were "the central events of his life. All of his subsequent poetry is referable in one way or another to these great decisions." (18) She reminds us that the wreck was a natural disaster and "sharpened in Hopkins's day by the impact of Darwinian doctrine of the struggle for existence, with 'nature red in the tooth and claw.'" (18) For the poet the disaster posed the dilemma of "whether he might not be guilty of loving material nature too passionately" over the claims of the spirit. (19)

Schneider goes on to heighten Hopkins's and the public's situation when she describes his ode as one where he proposes "the suggestion of a new miracle, the Scotus doctrine of Incarnation, the reconciliation of evil and suffering in the world with the Christian belief in an all-powerful, all-wise, all-good God." If we add to his Victorian era upbringing with its shallow conservatism, his unsupportive family's "terrible response," the conflict that "The Wreck" triggered, and the need of all initiates to prove themselves, Hopkins' conversion must have needed poetry to help convince himself of his faith and of his unique path in life. His conversion and his poetry put him "at war within." That war within was playing itself out in the era he represents in his poetry.

Hopkins' discovery of Duns Scotus' work is the impetus he needed to justify Christ to himself and to write the kind of poetry he was to write. Given the discovery, his poetry was going to need to be unconventional and against the poetic orthodoxy of the day. The discovery (invention really) of inscape and its necessary parts, instress, and sprung rhythm could not have been achieved without the push of desperation: How do I bring my faith and poetry together? It is almost humorous how Robert Bridges didn't recognize the innovation or was frightened of it. By "inscape" Hopkins means a complex of qualities that unites them to make something unique and different from other things. By "instress" he means either the energy within inscape that carries it into the mind of the beholder. For Hopkins, the energy seems to move from the beholder's mind and from God. The less metrical lines in sprung rhythm lead the reader to instress. The two-way nature of instress and inscape can be observed in his poem "God's Grandeur."

Today, we may read his poem "God's Grandeur," as a celebration of the durability of the planet. (*Gerard Manley Hopkins: The Major Works* Hopkins 2009: 128) However, Hopkins seems to be insisting on an instress that is charged both ways: His charge to God and God's to him, allowing him the perception or inscape he had. That two-way charge needs to be there for him; it can't be one way. The charge itself uses sprung rhythm to move the reader to the instress within the inscape. Iambic pentameter would have dulled the charge, made trivia of the experience the poet had and was sharing with the audience.

Perhaps it is desperation that is at the heart of each change in everything we do. We can add to Hopkins desperate need to prove his devotion to himself as a Catholic convert, Rorty's (1989) assertion here, an assertion that echoes T.S. Eliot's understanding of language:

> [R]evolutionary achievements in the arts, in the sciences, and in moral and political thought typically occur when somebody realizes that two or more of our vocabularies are interfering with each other, and proceeds to invent a new vocabulary to replace both. (*Contingency, Irony, and Solidarity* 1989: 12)

Or as he reminds us later in his book *Contingency, Irony, and Solidarity*:

> We shall see the conscious need of the strong poet to *demonstrate* that he is not a copy or replica as merely a special form of an unconscious need everyone has: the need to come to terms with the blind impress which chance has given him, to make a self for himself by redescribing the impress in terms which are, if only marginally, his own. (*Contingency, Irony, and Solidarity* 1989: 22)

Hopkins as a strong poet caught between two "vocabularies" proves through his invention that he was no "replica." His invention that is his idiosyncratic poetry is in keeping with William Blake's "I must create a system or be enslaved by another mans; I will not reason and compare: my business is to create." (Jerusalem, 1965, *The Poetry and Prose of William Blake* 1965: 151)

In his Italian sonnet "God's Grandeur" (2009) for instance, his argument in every line is charged, forced on the reader. The first quatrain describes the natural world as charged with God's presence as though with an electrical current. Hopkins finishes the quatrain as though he were proving God's presence and then asks how it is that man doesn't obey his authority. In the second quatrain, Hopkins describes the contemporary Victorian age as one staining with man's labor and becoming more and more spiritually alienated. In the sonnet, Hopkins' inscape is his evidence of God's presence in the world.

Here we have Hopkins representing the conflict of his age: The practice of science for commercial gain vs. religion. Here we have Hopkins desperate to argue religion's case and eventual victory over man's "smear." He uses instress to provoke the reader's mind to make that connection and see the insight, while the sprung rhythm (more common language than verse) assists in the provocation. The sestet asserts that even though the Victorian age has moved to embrace science and industry, nature (God's creation) continues to offer "freshness" by way of God's renewal. The last lines move from God's "brooding" promise to that of "ah! Bright wings" that fulfill the promise.

Hopkins uses the word "charged" to describe the instress he finds reaching out to him in the world. "The grandeur of God" is that charge as is the flaming, the shining and the oozing in the poem. The idea of "nature" in the poem is that of instress: God reaching out, and a man's ability to reach out also with an "ah" in recognition to make "bright wings" or "Holy Ghost," instress. (*Gerard Manley Hopkins: The Major Works* 2009: 128) His epiphanies, revelations, perceptions were fitting to a man searching for belief. His being able to write poetry to demonstrate his belief makes for unification for anyone religiously inclined. His need to break with the iamb and use sprung rhythm in the poem makes his poetry revolutionary in the Rortian sense and modern as it demonstrates that he is not a replica.

What makes Hopkins transitional is the metaphorical power of the image that grounds it in the contemporary world of the writer. Pound may have been influenced by the zeitgeist overlapping generations or a subconscious borrowing from Hopkins and secularizing inscape, instress, and sprung rhythm: Inscape, instress (without the religious baggage), and sprung rhythm's implied support for the idea of free verse. Even the *BLAST* manifesto mingles language of religion with the secular, the Victorian and the Modern. It doesn't take close examination to find in Imagism the ideas of inscape and instress. Simply the emphasis on the image tells us quite a bit: "The point of Imagisme is that it does not use images as ornaments. The image is itself the speech." (*Singing the Chaos* 1996: 131) However, Pound does instruct the writer also to write "in the stress of some emotion, [you] could actually say." (*The Marginalization of Poetry* Perelman1996: 43) William Pratt (1996) reminds us that

> Pounds' definition of image is close to the code of modernism in literature in that it seeks to fuse symbolism with realism to make an expressive vehicle of numinous perception, where ordinary sensations become imbued with extraordinary supersensory power. (*Singing the Chaos* 1996:131)

Notice how Pratt articulates the difference between Hopkins and modernism's image and instress: Not "supernatural power" for modernism but "supersensory power." It turns something religious or spiritual into something secular, human. Pratt goes on to draw convincing connections between inscape "the very soul of art" and Pounds' image, Joyce's epiphany, and Eliot's objective correlative. (*Singing the Chaos* 1996:40)

Further, Hugh Kenner reminds us when discussing "In a Station of the Metro" in his book *The Pound Era* (1971) that for Pound there was a formula that is often misunderstood for what he meant by Imagism: "Lord over fact." Pound called the formula an equation and wanted the Imagist poem to break "into some realm beyond the mood or the impression." (186) "For Pound's Imagism is energy, is effort. It does not appease itself by reproducing what is seen, but by setting some other seen thing in relation to it." (186) He came to describe the effect of the formula as Vorticism which includes "The vortex is the point of maximum energy. It represents, in mechanics, the greatest efficiency." (www.poetryfoundation.org/learning/essay/238700) Pound's energy is similar if not the same as what Hopkins meant by instress though they were bringing insight from different symbolic orders: Greek for Pound and Catholic for Hopkins.

The idea of "lord over fact" for Pound and Lord over fact for Hopkins is important to what I am suggesting regarding the secularization (or creating metaphor) for what Hopkins saw as a religious Lord and literal. For Pound the idea of "lord" was that it (the symbol) controlled the contemporary image. Kenner puts it this way when explaining the simile with the "like" suppressed in the poem "In the Station of the Metro," "Pound called it an equation, meaning not a redundancy, a equals a, but a generalization of unexpected exactness." (185) Pound in his attempt to find the "it" in "make it new" was attempting to recover or remind us that the values and ideas of the past (Greek) were present though twisted in the current day and readers should be aware of their significance. Those "apparitions" in the subway were for Pound the figures seen by Odysseus and Orpheus in Hades, while the poem also connects us to the *hokku* of the Japanese tradition. In some sense Pound may be our first multi-cultural poet. (184)

Whether Pound read Hopkins and recognized the value of Hopkins' invention or whether the Enlightenment zeitgeist of the day was on either of their minds, Pound was reacting to the same issue Baudelaire and Hopkins were reacting to: The demise of religion and tradition. Hopkins' reaction was an attempt to create a fortress around what he thought was Christian, while Pound attempted to save what was of value in the aristocratic traditions of the West and the world. Both poets realized that the natural object is an adequate symbol and as Donald Davie points out in *Ezra Pound* (1975), "'the luminous detail,' the single particular which, chosen with enough care and rendered with enough exactness, can impel the reader to summon up for himself all the other particulars implied by that salient one." (36) We can say this of Hopkins' poetry as well. In "God's Grandeur" for example, we find his use of natural objects and salient particulars that result in the instresses of the inscape for the reader. Hopkins brings the reader in contact with the natural world and the religious world in his other sonnets as well.

In Pound's formula "lord over fact," he is using lord metaphorically to undercut modernity's fascination with facts found in images. (Notice how "formula" or "equation" is itself language readily available via Enlightenment lexicon. Modernist artists seem to have an inferiority complex around science and thus often use its vocabulary to legitimize their work.) Hopkins uses lord literally to remind or reassure Victorian England that Christianity transcended artificial laminations found in facts. Hopkins' poems were reminders of the images to embrace nature beneath the facts of the Victorian Age. Pound uses the equation to charge the foreground with the wisdom of the ancient civilizations while Hopkins uses his invention (another word from the Enlightenment lexicon) to call forth Christian symbolism. Both poets require the energy created in the lord or lording over fact. The allusion to ancients requires the energy of the reader as does the allusions to Christianity. The connotations alert the reader to worlds (Christian and ancient Greek) beyond modernity.

Even if the poet were to lord the "fact" as the iconoclast William Carlos Williams does, inscape and instress are evident. His going after the particular thing as in "The Red Wheelbarrow" and the particular experience in "This Is Just to Say" celebrate the stripping of connotation, the uniqueness of the object or experience and their fleeting nature. To do so his poems rest on instressed images within inscapes. His poems hold the tension of his age in their mourning. It is important to add that just as Pound and

Eliot moved to Europe to escape the lack of tradition in America (and attempt to save the "mind of Europe," Williams embraced the iconoclasm, the opportunity to start over in an attempt to democratize the English language. But just as Pound and Eliot carried cultural emptiness to Europe, Williams carries Hopkins and imagism without even having to go to Europe. Both branches of the modernist movement owe quite a bit to the ideas that Hopkins embraced.

In the works by the modernists, we easily find their mourning, the loss of tradition. One only needs to read what is being responded to in their works. Pound in "The Return" mourns the lack of "the leash-men" as he mourns throughout the *Cantos*. Eliot shores fragments of the past classics against his (and for him, our) ruin in "The Wasteland." Yeats (1974) yearns to be a golden bird "To keep a drowsy Emperor awake." (*The Collected Poems of W. B. Yeats* 1974: 191) Frost's "The Road Not Taken" mourns the loss of companionship and "The Death of the Hired Man" mourns the loss of the agrarian life. One reads Stevens' "Sunday Morning," and it is clear the loss of God marks the century. It isn't until we read Camus or Beckett that the attitude changes to a celebration of the absurd. For Camus it is in his essays but all through Beckett's novels, poems, and plays we have the comic, the absurd presenting something new: The serious playing, the honest joke that is on us all.

I want to move ahead now to an English woman who became American and wrote modern poetry that was pushing itself toward the postmodern. Denise Levertov was a follower of Ezra Pound and William Carlos Williams and a friend of Robert Duncan. I think that I can use one example of her poetry and we may be able to see her debt to Hopkins and how she makes Hopkins' instress new. First, in her article "Some Notes on Organic Form" (1965) written for *Poetry Magazine*, she advocates allowing the poem to determine the form it takes, moving beyond Hopkins and one could argue modernism. She addresses her subject in Hopkinsean terms.

> I would speak of *the inscape of an experience* (Which might be composed of any and all of these elements, including the sensory) or of the inscape of a sequence or constellation of experiences…First there must be an experience a sequence or constellation of perception of sufficient interest felt by the poet intensely enough to demand of him their equivalence in words: he is *brought to speech*. (*Poetry Magazine* 1965: 420-425)

One might be tempted to see here even the instress as Hopkins defines it in the idea of being "*brought to speech*," but notice the shift from object to experience. The article is an attempt to use Hopkins' inventions as a springboard to other inventions or stretching his inventions to rationalize projective verse: "Form is never more than a *revelation* of content." (*Poetry Magazine* 1965: 424) It is the distrust of form as "nostalgia for the impossible" that makes projectivism flirt with postmodernism. (*The Postmodern Explained* Lyotard 1992: 15) However, William Wordsworth's emphasis on memory for composition of poetry can also be seen.

The title of her poem "The Charge" in her 1958 book *With Eyes at the Back of Our Heads* may say all that needs saying about her debt to Hopkins, but she has turned his "charged" into a pun of several understandings. On the one hand the word is the power of Hopkins' instress as "The world is charged..." on the other hand she is announcing her duty as a poet, especially as it is the second poem in the book. However, perhaps even charge as accusation and charge as replenishment, as in charging a battery may work in writing poetry for Levertov. Of course, the word implies all of these understandings.

Levertov's poem seems to tell the reader that the charge for Levertov is to use her memory to compose inscapes from instresses (charges) by following the projectivist charge: Envision the page as a field where one perception immediately and directly leads to a further perception. Each perception is a charge, an instress. (Notice that the title of the book is a looking back. Walter Benjamin's idea of the angel of history comes to mind.) She states, "Returning / to all the unsaid / all the lost living...and dead" that she only celebrates in dreams that are ghosts by morning. (*With Eyes at the Back of Our Heads* 1958: 11) We can see by the line breaks and indentations that Levertov is using the page as a field upon which to lead us in interpretation, helping us to see the instresses as moves across the field and through the poem. Because she is following Pound's advice that poetry should read as prose, sprung rhythm isn't necessary to bring out instress or to heighten the inscape. The poem almost literally points out what Hopkins called "the soul of art." In manifesto-like advice, she gives voice to the ghosts and instructs "make / my image. Let be / what is gone." (*With Eyes at the Back of Our Heads* 1958: 11) Her charge seems to be one as old as inspiration. So much about this poem teeters between mourning and celebration.

These images or perceptions were not religious in nature of course. (However, one could argue that the Christian tradition is imbedded in the framework, since Levertov admits being influenced by Hopkins.) Projectivist poets followed the objectivists who in turn followed the imagists and thus the lineage. What is a perception for Hopkins and projectivists but the charge imbedded in revelatory images? Projectivism becomes postmodernism when one applies Eliot's warning: The meaning of a poem is only "to keep the [reader's] mind diverted and quiet while the poem does its work upon him: Much as the imaginary burglar is always provided with a bit of meat for the house-dog." (*Singing the Chaos* 1996: 42)

Eliot may have been suggesting tricking the house-dog for psychological reasons to create objective correlatives to cure Europe. However, it is when using this tool that the postmodern poet can push away from cliché meanings, mainstream ideology, and wisdom (often with the use of irony) when writing poetry. The instresses or perceptions don't have to have a psychological realism to compose a whole. Often the poem is made up of ironic instresses. The poems often create impasses (aporia) presenting what the modernist would leave out. In fact, the ironic linkages in these poems often move the reader through the poem.

It may be time to attempt to define postmodernism as best as I am able. (Fredric Jameson avoids a definition or its rules.) Though the postmodern has sometimes been defined as a period, Jean-Francois Lyotard in his suggestion for understanding it states that sometimes a work first has to be postmodern before it can be modern. He goes on to suggest that postmodernism can manifest through "the power of the faculty to conceive, through what one might call its 'inhumanity' (a quality Apollinaire insists on in modern artists)." Here he is suggesting that the artist is celebrating the imagination's ability to "invent new rules of the game." (*The Postmodern Explained*, Lyotard 1992: 13) Later Wittgenstein writings can be seen in this understanding of postmodern as embracing the idea of language games. However, Lyotard also brings in another element of the postmodern when he states the following:

> The postmodern would be that which in the modern invokes the unpresentable in the presentation itself, that which refuses the consolation of correct forms, refuses the consensus of taste permitting a common experience of nostalgia for the impossible, and inquires into new presentation – not to take pleasure in them, but to better produce the feeling that there is something unpresentable. (*The Postmodern Explained* Lyotard 1992:15)

If the modern poet's role was once one of serious unification, a momentary stay through reason against confusion, postmodern poetry is a momentary *play* against reason, changing first the poet's attitude from one of desperation to one of serious play in questioning, problematizing, reformulating, and presenting "other," the "unpresentable in the presentation itself." (*The Sublime* Shaw 2006: 116) The exposed "unpresentable" is often referred to as the "other," the feminine sublime. The postmodern attitude even opens Frost's bid for unity or order in his essay to play and suggests that his poetry as emblematic of modern poetry and is open for play also. But why would postmodernists want to play against reason with such serious matters as technological change at hand? They are convinced that the world and a human's relationship to it, the one of development and progress are absurd. It is also reason that brought the West grand narratives that led us to Holocaust, Hiroshima, and global capitalism.

Since Hopkins and Pound understood that an image must present "an intellectual and emotional complex in an instant of time" and let us not forget Pounds' call to "make it new," postmodernism's attitude of play makes perfect sense. (*Singing the Chaos* Pratt 1996: 140) While Pound's call lacks the references to ancient Greece, postmodernism uses what Gilles Deleuze calls "new weapons" from his "Postscript on the Societies of Control" to resist the cliché, the platitude disguising as a thought. (https://files.nyu.edu/dnm232/public/deleuze_postcript.pdf) The complex within imagery demands a maturity or stress that brings realism and symbolism together in new ways, ways that bring pause and pondering not pause with satisfaction. Postmodern art in general attempts to engage and include the reader in the play. One might think that contemporary poetry is made up of what Fredric Jameson might call politically unconscious poets who are stuck in mainstream ideology and poets who play with language at the expense of ideology to make room for new thoughts, poets who inspired Charles Bernstein's book (2011), *The Attack of Difficult Poetry*.

The "play" is the different ways to jolt the mainstream ideological poets from their conventions to recognize the limits of their convention, the political consequences to others of that limitation, and where possibility for something different may begin. I can't emphasis the last point enough. Postmodern poetry can be a threshold, an exit from the ideology currently playing itself out through capitalism. Northrop Frye (1964) warns, especially to poets, that "[p]eople who can do nothing but accept their social mythology [ideology] can only try to huddle more closely together when they feel frightened or threatened, and in that situation their clichés turn hysterical." (*Educated Imagination* 1964: 146) Blake (1965) put it this way in "The Marriage of Heaven and Hell: "one law for the lion & ox is oppression." (*The Poetry and Prose of William Blake*: 43) I bring this up because the reader needs to remember inscape and instress as the ties to modernism and Hopkins when reading postmodern poetry. It may also be useful to remember that even Hopkins' inventions are open to that "play." The poem we will consider falls into that category.

The following poem "Magnificat for the New Year" (2011) by Sheila Murphy (no relation) may serve to identify the postmodern qualities about which I have been writing. I may have chosen a more noted poet such as John Ashbery. However, a member of a younger generation of poets will do well also. Sheila uses subtle irony, to create the "complex" of intellect and emotion. The reader will recognize irony in the words scat and four-four time, festoons and staves, reflex and obedience, neighborly non sequiturs, hinges and awareness, legato and imperatives, and winter roses. There are other examples of course. The irony throws the reader into making meaning, thus reminding the reader that disorder / aporia (what Jean-Francois Lyotard calls feminine sublime) is present and involving the reader in the creative process.

**Magnificat for the New Year**

Scat-sung cadenzas festoon open staves
in feasts transcending four-four time.

A curvature of instinct rescues selves
from the erosive reflex of obedience.

We rise to the occasion of each other,
toward a more palpable compassion.

In a world of neighborly non sequiturs,
we celebrate new hinges of awareness.

Legato moments lift into syllabic flight,
resilient pathways to imperatives.

The body's best defense, unbroken skin,
a hush of snow light upon winter roses (Postcard: 2011).

The title of the poem should give us plenty to use as a foundation for the poem. The title "Magnificat for the New Year" promises us that below the title is a poem celebrating for the new year and wishing to be understood as a canticle of the Virgin Mary, a celebration of the Virgin and women singing her praises. However the first two-lined sentence suggests that the scat singing opens staves by sagging them and violating a song's time. With the irony in those images, disorder threatens, the irrational seems to be in the song of praise. The "curvature" in the next line echoes the festoon and tells the reader that the making of disorder is instinctual and something to celebrate in women who also have an urge toward "obedience." The poem thus sets up a holiday from the rhythms of life (not to be mistaken for confusion) by presenting in the writing itself the struggle between spontaneity and regularity that is outlined in the rescue from obedience by scat singing.

We find Hopkins in the use of inscape, the celebration of an unconventional magnificat sung by a woman's choir celebrating women. The instresses may be found, for instance, in the irony in the "Scat-sung cadenzas," and "A curvature of instinct" that rescues the song and the women. Each is a perception that leads to a further perception, the method that Hopkins and Levertov use. The poem goes on to suggest that the benefit of the syncopation that breaks up regularity and convention is a more acceptable compassion, a freer choice toward neighborliness. Hopkins uses sprung rhythm in a similar way, to break convention and heighten statements. An ordinary day would have a neighborhood made up of separate people, individuals of different interests and different motives and not the common urban/suburban scene of "hello" in the morning and that is all. The poem praises compassion with a sensuously feminine celebratory connotation and tone. However, because the poem is made up of perceptions, images or instresses that use syncopated rhythms to drive an inscape to the reader's sensibility (not to mention its celebration of Jesus' mother, Mary), Hopkins invention is evident and made new with innovation.

To illustrate the breadth of my assertion, we might look at poems by poets such as Arthur Vogelsang. For the sake of a second example, I have chosen "The Writers" from his book *Left Wing of a Bird*. However, we could choose any of the poems. In "The Writers," Vogelsang seems to use a Jungian yin-yang notion of gender. The poem is broken into two parts; the second half is in quotations and is a woman's voice. In fact, not only is the persona's voice fragmented but the poem is made of fragments suggesting that the writer of the poem is "loco with a motive" (9) and therefore even fragmenting the word locomotive in the first line of the poem. He puns with the word "plane" so that meaning is fragmented. The men mentioned are fragmented "crippled." (9) The poem even suggests that the fragmentation careens and that a fragmented culture careens.

The second half of the poem speaks of a "burned torn book," "a quarrel," "sleeping together but apart," and woman who seems to also be a part of the narrator. The woman's voice even suggests that she is fragmented. Her thighs and her hair "Seemed separate from me // As if hanging in a butcher's shop // Or in a Native American window in New York." (10) The violence is apparent enough to suggest that of the nation itself broken into states and reservations. The poem moves back to nothing to read and nothing to write, the sad movement being buried in ellipsis . . . sheets of paper. "The Writers," as does Murphy's poem, depends on a series of ironic perceptions or instresses that depend on the reader to link into an inscape. The inscape (often an enormous insight) makes up whatever meaning can be constructed from the debris, the fragments with aporia between.

The postmodern poet wants to first acknowledge contingency, unpredictable change to remind the audience (or better yet participants) that there are alternative directions in which to move. It is here that one is reminded also that the only conventions we have are the ones we make, together. Attempting to hold worlds together or creating utopia, is not of interest. The postmodern wishes to interrogate, qualify, expose difference in grand narratives. It leans toward the ephemeral, toward the Now and then Now as the sublime and the gaps, aporia, and contingency embrace that "now," that sublime. The poet recognizes the value of play as a strategy to allow and expect contingency and to problematize perspectives to keep open possibility and to check narratives of religion, reason, and technology. To trouble perspectives in art is to bring discomfort to set forms of thinking, but artists want to problematize as an exercise to reveal or to remind one of possibilities and open minds to other forms of thought. Poets play by fragmentizing, creating gaps, making use of irony, aporia, paradox, and counter-intuitive notions. Often bringing two languages from different fields together create this kind of sublime. It is hoped that the result is to involve the reader in the creative process. A postmodern poem's title is a call to come out and play in an effort to enrich the mind and emotions.

So what connects Murphy's, Vogelsang's poems and many other postmodern poetic efforts to Hopkins? Inscape: even if the poet attempts to keep the inscape open, without a close. There is a perspective being given, and within it, several. The larger perspective lacks orthodoxy and a commitment to any dogma. It is attempting to bring into the perspective the complications of that perspective, the irony involved in the line of thought, where assumptions are truly gaps. Sprung rhythm is in the free verse that delivers the instresses. Instresses are the irony, the gaps, and complications and not the absolutism in a perspective. Here the poets know Eliot's warning regarding meaning in a poem. So while Hopkins was using both the meaning and the "work" of the poem to bring unity to his belief in Catholicism, his reader desired unity. Because the West moved into Enlightenment thinking, through the World Wars, and now into the information age, at least briefly, the moods and attitudes of the populations have changed and continue to do so, quickly. First the West suffered desperation at the threat of losing unity; then it mourned a loss of unity (while art provided momentary stays against confusion); and today it celebrates the post-Enlightenment play, the balancing act of freedom and responsibility. However, variations on Hopkins' invention threads poetry's ax handles.

## WORKS CITED

Bernstein, Charles. *The Attack of the Difficult Poem*. Chicago: University of Chicago Press, 2002.
Davie, Donald. *Ezra Pound*. New York: Viking Press, 1975.
Deleuze, Gilles. "Postscript on the Societies of Control." New York University, https://files.nyu.edu/dnm232/public/deleuze_postcript.pdf.
Erdman, David V., ed. *The Poetry and Prose of William Blake*. "Jerusalem." New York: Doubleday, 1965.
———. *The Poetry and Prose of William Blake*. "The Marriage of Heaven and Hell." New York: Doubleday, 1965.
Frost, Robert. "The Figure a Poem Makes." *Collected Poems of Robert Frost*. New York: Holt, Rhinehart, & Winston, 1939.
Frye, Northrop. *The Educated Imagination*. Bloomington: Indiana University Press, 1964.
Hopkins, Gerard Manley. *Gerard Manley Hopkins: The Major Works*. 128. Oxford: Oxford World Classics, 2009.
Kenner, Hugh. *The Pound Era*. University of California Press, 1971.
Levertov, Denise. *With Eyes at the Back of Our Heads*. New York: New Directions, 1958.
———. "Some Notes on Organic Form." *Poetry*, vol. 106, no. 6, Sep. 1965, pp. 420-25.
Lyotard, Jean-Francois. *The Postmodern Explained*, Translated by Julian Pefanis and Morgan Thomas. Minneapolis: University of Minnesota Press, 1992.
Murphy, Sheila. "Magnificat for the New Year." New Year postcard distributed by author, 2011.
Perelman, Bob. *The Marginalization of Poetry*. Princeton: Princeton University Press, 1996.
Phillips, Catherine. *Gerard Manley Hopkins: The Major Works*. Oxford World's Classics, Oxford: Oxford University Press, 2009.

CHAPTER 5

## "Vexed to Nightmare by a Rocking Cradle": Ginsberg's Performativity

My paper will draw on Michel Foucault's insight into the nature of discourse and in particular the unstable nature of discourse that sometimes reinforces power and knowledge and that sometimes acts as a "hindrance or stumbling-block" to power and knowledge. Foucault's nuanced difference between "deploying sexuality" and "deploying alliance" may shed light on the acts of the poem and Ginsberg's lifetime. (*History of Sexuality,* 101) (106) For Foucault deploying alliance was to seek or give spoken or unspoken allegiance to kinship with its rules regarding marriage and family in an effort to maintain a stable social structure. Deployment of sexuality is less restrictive and more varied and includes a range of sexual behavior and pleasure. Foucault maintains that alliance deployed first and that sex evolved from alliance.

    This paper will also use selected vocabulary and ideas of Erving Hoffman in *The Presentation of Self in Everyday Life* to imagine the motive for Ginsberg's writing of the poem and for the acting out of Ginsberg's life into the performance of a unique role for his time. The paper also calls attention to two basic speech-acts as defined by J.L. Austin as either "constative" (descriptive) and "performative" (performing an act) when Ginsberg constructs contrast within "Howl." (*How to Do Things with Words* 3)

    The poem is often referred to as visionary in that visionary poetry presents the reader clear and insightful images that create an ideal, even if the image is dystopic so that the reader needs to surmise the opposite. The results may be "insights into spiritual reality by a mystic in trance or ecstasy." (*The New Princeton Encyclopedia* 1359) The visionary lens as interpreted by Coleridge is broken into two types of visions: secondary and primary imaginations (in the order stated here). The second being one that Coleridge used (analysis and then creativity) and the primary imagination is one religious mystics used to bring the authority of a god into their writing. (516) Ginsberg's "first word, best word" strategy seems to derive from the primary imagination approach to poetry. This approach takes great naiveté or a very large narcissism.

    "Howl" has been a part of the American and world cultural tradition for 60 years. Allen Ginsberg has been dead for 18 years and yet poets, and anyone interested in culture, continue to meet and discuss the poem as well as the life and times of the poet. This paper makes the argument that due to the nightmare era that gave birth to the holocaust and the world war of Ginsberg's upbringing, his influence by a poet father and by an emotionally disturbed mother, Ginsberg's performance skills as poet and public figure brought him fame as a poet too soon. However, the strong performance gave shape to the counter-culture. By way of the lenses by various thinkers of the idea of performance and literature, this paper is an attempt at sneaking back stage or lurking behind the scenes of Ginsberg's writing performance when writing "Howl." It is also an attempt at considering the performance of his life and why it may have been more important than any one of his poems.

## Performing "Howl"

The structure of "Howl" is said to be modernist and one influenced by Whitman's longer line and attitude and by Blake's visionary poetry. This may be true. However, as a written performance, "Howl" has a structure and complaint that also resembles poems written that could have been written by some of the English World War I poets. This poet can easily imagine Wilfred Owen, Siegfried Sassoon, or Herbert Read writing the longer line and using repetition in a poem to drive the suffering of soldiers. The poem's catalog nature and timing, written after both world wars, would lead one to expect a poem about the loss of generations of best minds in the young men that were killed in the fighting in each war or both. One could catalog in a very convincing way the loss of the Jewish generations from 1900 to 1945 in Europe. (An imaginative person would be in awe to think what those minds might have contributed to Europe during that time. That too is a very big loss.) One may expect that from the nightmare of both world wars that rocked a cultural cradle, global shell shock or post-traumatic stress disorder would follow.

The historical situation that Ginsberg found himself in was not lost on him. In John Raskin's book *American Scream*, he tells us that in his youth Ginsberg "was astounded to learn that in Germany and in Italy political parties advocated 'killing all the Jews'" (34). Raskin goes on to say that "given the geopolitical and personal backdrop of Allen's early development, it's understandable that he grew up to write the poetry of personal crack-up and political catastrophe" (34). Conscious or not about the self-proclamation that thrust him into the world of American poetry, he could be understood as having been reacting to the pressures of his day, a new voice emerging with force within American culture. The voice is one of pain but also one of celebration that made Ginsberg a hero.

It has been suggested convincingly that the poem may have been written in response to Louis Simpson's and other veterans' war poetry. At Columbia, Ginsberg had been in poetry workshops with WWII veterans who were writing about their experiences. One can easily imagine that Ginsberg may have felt his non-veteran experiences at home being dwarfed or made insignificant in comparison to the experiences portrayed in the veterans' poems. A natural reaction by someone who had suffered what Ginsberg suffered as a child at home would be to write about the troubles State-side at home and in his vicinity. No one likes being discounted or ignored, especially if the suffering experienced was real and significant. Ginsberg's and his friends' sufferings were significant. While the soldiers certainly suffered, many Americans suffered at home also.

Majorie Perloff in writing about "Howl" reminds readers of not only the difference between what poetry was being written and published when Ginsberg performed and published his poem but that he was in workshop classes with WWII veterans at Columbia. She later writes:

> Ginsberg…was probably a much truer Modernist than were mandarin poets like Louis Simpson or Donald Hall. Indeed, Ginsberg had so thoroughly internalized the aesthetic of the Modernists…that Howl unwittingly makes the case of *showing* rather than *telling*, for the inseparability of *form* and *content* and even for Cleanth Brooks's theorem that "the language of poetry is the language of paradox." (30)

Her observation and insight help us understand where the attention of poets was directed when he was at Columbia and after and what Ginsberg had absorbed as a young poet. It isn't a reach from there to his need for attention that veterans were receiving. After all, he was a veteran of the domestic horror of such acts as standing in as a child for his father and taking (alone) his mother on public transportation to the nursing facility for her insanity. His acting out, as a psychologist might say, his performance both at Columbia by being expelled and in the writing of "Howl" where he demands attention were what made his poem new. So new that M. L, Rosenthal remarked, "that he has brought a terrible psychological reality to the surface with enough originality to blast American verse a hairsbreadth forward in the process." (30)

The poem's Part I is a catalog of men or a catalog of composites of men who Ginsberg claims make up the best minds of a generation in America, and they are not the minds of soldiers who fought during WWII necessarily but the minds of men who may have been called the insane by a large segment of the audience in the 1950s. His catalog of men on the fringe of society struggling against a child-eating beast was written before Michel Foucault wrote his book *History of Madness*. Understanding this puts into perspective the "unpresentable" boundary that the poem crosses in its presentation and performance. By speaking of the unspeakable, it crosses the boundary that made up the limitations of American mainstream ideology and decorum.

Ginsberg touches on presenting the unpresentable when he commented:

> I'm not concerned with creating a work of art…And I don't want to predefine it…what I do is try to forget entirely about the whole world of art and just get directly to the…fastest and most direct expression of what it is I got in heart-mind. Trusting that if my heart-mind is shapely, the objects or words, the word sequences, the sentences, the lines, the song, will also be shapely. (115)

John Tytell calls attention to Ginsberg's ideal poem as "notation of undifferentiated consciousness." (178) The reader may also question his use of language that often lacks syntax and pairs nouns. What pushes readers to pause when reading the long lines in a rhythmic way is the aporia caused by juxtaposition of the words themselves. The presentation of aporia is expected in the postmodern poem. It is its sublime moments. Were those strategies purposeful "first thought best thought" in an attempt to create aporia or were they accidental aporia? "Howl's" lack of irony, its presentation of Ginsberg as having a "devout acceptance of himself dispensing with false modesty and self-deprecation," and its composition as modernist in principal as Marjorie Perloff points out may make it a modern poem that stumbles occasionally into post-modernism.

In addition, when reading "Howl," its tone is not one that reminds this reader of Whitman or of a Blake. "Howl" has the tone of complaint with little celebration as in Whitman or the hope of a New Jerusalem as in Blake. The poem lampoons aspects of American culture with frustration, suffering, and legitimate anger using lingo from the streets, literature, and bible. On the one hand the poem tempts the reader to take what it presents seriously and at the same time seems as though it should be addressing a young, simply restless audience. It is that dual use of language that confuses some conservative adult readers while attracting young readers interested in experiments.

Many readers have mentioned how the poem lacks decorum or how it "deliberately assaults and inverts it readers' assumptions about what is holy or hellish, sane or mad." (Gates 161) Here an understanding of "acting out" will be useful in order to understand the poem as a performance. Acting out, when deliberately used by psychologists on a patient to re-enact or to practice new behavior, can be seen as helpful and have positive results for the doctor and perhaps the patient who may wish to achieve general alliance with his society. However, acting out is in a general sense categories of specific behaviors that allow the professional and the conformed adult to label someone who is acting out of character, usually to manipulate the behavior and often the person performing the behavior. Goffman defines conforming as the following:

> When an actor takes on an established social role, usually he finds that the particular front has already been established for it. Whether his acquisition of the role was primarily motivated by a desire to perform the given task of by a desire to maintain the corresponding front, the actor will find that he must do both. (7)

In fact, Ginsberg's father had suggested to Allen, "[you have] developed intellectually; but, emotionally, you lag," and in light that the poem is personal (confessional) and has often been called a rant, the term acting out may serve me. (Breslin 411) I am using the concept such as it is for the performance of his poem and for the performance of his life. Whether Ginsberg lagged emotionally or not, he created a new shape to a "social front" as Goffman would say. (26) He added depth to a bohemian front and merged it with those marginalized by way of their madness, drug use, homosexuality, and opposition to capitalism. With a handful of other spokespeople performing similarly at that time, a counter-culture was created, a culture that opposed mainstream culture for nearly 20 years.

Acting out is always a spectacle in the minds of adults whose minds have conformed to state and mainstream ideology and perhaps now even having a great stake in their conformity. Acting out may be seen as a kind of graffiti, graphic by nature, making it unpresentable in the eyes of those who have conformed, the middleclass occupant with lots to lose. The poem itself may have been a written form of acting out that Ginsberg continued in his public performances for many years. Richard Elman reminds us that "his acting out became a way of perceiving his adversity and, through genius, overcoming it." (329) In any case, the poem's and Ginsberg's performance of "genuine suffering" would be one on the fringe of symbolic order that makes up the primary code of mainstream ideology, creating disorientation, aporia. (31)

The poem is broken into three parts and a fourth called "Footnote." The first part that contains for this reader a false note, lays out the complaint, the problem. Again, the list that makes up the first part could just as easily be a list of soldiers who died in trenches or a list of Jews who weren't able to escape the death camps. The second part assigns guilt and responsibility, and the third part resolves to declare, to perform where the poet stands. The Footnote attempts to connect the three sections to the spiritual realm. The poem is referred to as visionary because Ginsberg chanted the poem when he performed it. However, visionary is most often prophetic in its telling the reader what usually happens given a certain set of circumstances, not merely what happened. In addition, a postmodern visionary poem would not lean on history or religious mythology; it would need to find its integrity in the shallow historical moment of the poem itself. This is important to keep in mind going forward.

Part I of the poem is one of a catalog constate, describing the minds that had been "destroyed by madness." (9) In each description he is advocating deployment of sexuality against alliance but recording basic injustices or the penalties assigned to the victims. Each person or composite described is active and often deploying sexuality; each sat, dreamed, copulated, wandered, etc., except one where the composite "lost their loveboys" (14). This is a powerful segment in the poem because the language sets up a kind of injustice and the audience expects to have identified the guilty party or parties of the injustice. Ginsberg's compression of language in "the heterosexual dollar" is charged and effective. (One thinks of Foucault's powerful use of language.) It brings out the dominator's system, power and knowledge, the alliance that includes mainstream ideology that is responsible for the cultural, political, and economic situation of most of the people who Ginsberg is describing.

If he had used that concept of heterosexual dollar and left it at that, his poem would have more fully succeeded as a visionary poem (in Coleridge's secondary imagination category), a visionary poem with postmodern characteristics. His vision in this poem is not a new one however. His poem does not enlighten the reader as to the cause of suffering with insightful reasoning of his day. In fact, it leans on an old patriarchal ideology that goes back to Adam, so that it unconsciously deploys advocacy of alliance. (Foucault, History of Sexuality, 106) It does not act as a "hindrance or stumbling-block" but reinforces power and knowledge. (Foucault 101) He does admit on June 14, 1966 at a special Senate Subcommittee on his drug experiences that "drugs had helped him overcome stereotypes of habit by releasing inner and latent resources of feeling for other human beings, especially women." I interpret this admission as one that may apply to the shrews in "Howl," limiting its insight as a visionary poem and promoting the cliché ideology that has controlled our lives for millennia. It is also evidence that Coleridge's secondary imagination was not a strong force in the composing of the poem.

His three shews appear to this reader to be 1950s house wives dressed in ancient Greek mythology. By having the first one-eyed shrew (or fate) be of the "heterosexual dollar" he seems to be suggesting that she is the U.S. Treasury, in charge of the house money one might say. The second shrew who "winks out of the womb" as perhaps a seductress, seems to suggest that she invites helpless men in. The third shrew really makes the case for the stereotypical 50s housewife without bonbons by using the stereotype "that does nothing but / sit on her ass and snip the intellectual golden / threads of the craftsman's loom." (14) I understand that the suggestion may be that many gay men deployed alliance as a way to appear legitimate in an ideology that labeled them insane, as having hormonal deficiency, and criminals. The practice of deploying alliance remains with us even today, even with greater sexual and gender liberation, and isn't gay marriage merely a new deployment of alliance for the heterosexual dollar?

However, his poem's thrust misses the mark. Instead of blaming a fellow victim of the power-knowledge discourse of the day, Ginsberg might have made headway into making his poem a truly visionary work by hitting the mark with his blame: Heterosexual ideology, men pledging heterosexuality to settle a matter of sexuality and gender, not women whose minds one could argue were being destroyed in vastly greater numbers than those in Ginsberg's poem. Even advocating the liberation of women would have assisted the argument that the poem was making. One might argue that he was a product of the fifties and modernism so he wasn't privy to our thinking. However, that is precisely what makes one question whether this poem is a visionary postmodern poem and question whether it deploys bad ideology if one is interested in liberation. In any case, Ginsberg's moving beyond blaming the heterosexual dollar to blame women may be troublesome for anyone reading the poem from 1970 on and especially insightful women.

The constate speech act that makes up Part I of the poem in Part II declares that the situation these minds find themselves in is the fault of Moloch, the child eating biblical beast. Calling Moloch the sphinx (that the Greeks often thought of as a woman) "of cement and aluminum who bashed their skulls and ate their brains and imagination," Ginsberg now truly points the finger. (21) He identifies and describes the villain or villainess. Though much of his descriptive list of characteristics seem understandable up to the "sensitive bullshit," and at times he seems to be suggesting an ideology ("I am consciousness without my body"), had he not mentioned the shrews, the fates, I would not have understood the sphinx as necessarily a woman. So, my mind returns to Part I for connection and finds the capitalist, "winking," and "snipping" shrews of fate as at least in league with Moloch if not one and the same. (22) Beyond that, where are the nurturers and protectors of those children under stairs who had their brains and imaginations eaten? They are not mentioned. If one were to follow the poem's logic, mother was not performing her cultural alliance duty and perhaps father wasn't either. Is Moloch mother or the patriarchy?

It is Part III of the poem where its language is performative. "Carl Solomon! I am with you in Rockland / where you are madder than I am" is performative in its empathetic gesture, its solidarity with a man in an asylum. (24) The performance is persistent in its stating "I am with you in Rockland" 18 more times in the poem. (24) The performance seems one of giving legitimacy to those considered to be insane, outside mainstream ideology outside power and knowledge. Ginsberg then is using his role as a poet, a troubadour, and "legislator of the world" to call attention to the plight of the homosexual, the institutionalized, the anti-capitalists, and the marginalized populations and to legitimize them as humans struggling as workers. Thus his reference to "The Internationale:" "Tis the final conflict / Let us unite tomorrow, / The International / Will be the human race." (Eugene Pottier) Here again the military/militant imagery echoes.

If the poem's inversion (of heaven and hell) wasn't clear in the three parts, the Footnote makes it clear that the "bum's as holy as the seraphim," as is the "asshole," "typewriter," and "the vast lamb of the middleclass!" (27-28) Again, without regard for decorum and mainstream ideology, in an attempt to break alliance for the reader, the poet is "after the poem as discovered in the mind and in the process of writing it out on the page as notes, transcriptions." (Perloff 31) I suppose if Ginsberg was attempting to revive the poet as visionary prophet and attempting to produce a vision via primary imagination, this strategy may be one road to try, but the poem reaches back and not forward. His lack of control over his shaping of the content of the poem makes for his considering poetry secondary to giving voice to a prophet as history knew him. Because it reaches back for its vision, it is not a postmodern visionary poem.

## PERFORMING ALLEN GINSBERG AS COUNTER-CULTURE ICON

All this said, one can't separate the sexuality from the poem. In 1957, Ginsberg and Ferlinghetti were sued for obscenities. In his book *Allen Ginsberg,* Thomas Merrill tells us, "If nothing else, the legal proceedings brought against 'Howl' for obscenity served to make it easily one of the bestselling volumes of poetry of the twentieth century." Ginsberg and Ferlinghetti won the law suit, and in an article in the *San Francisco Chronicle*, Lawrence Ferlinghetti remarked that the trial rendered the book famous and aided in the sale of 10,000 copies (Merrill 51). Ginsberg's being a Jew when declaring sexual liberation ten years after the Holocaust of WWII complicated efforts by the courts or anyone else to quiet him. The West shared in great guilt or one state thrusted it onto the others.

Ginsberg's confessional poem was three years prior to Robert Lowell's confession of his father's and his culture's failure in his "groundbreaking" *Life*

*Studies.* Ginsberg' confessional style was instrumental in establishing his heroism. Ginsberg's Whitmanesque metrically free loose verse with its long line also mocked the tight academic poetry that ruled the small, elite poetry audience of the day. The powerful effect of Ginsberg being a Jew after WWII confessing his beat fate and that of friends in a poem can't be overstated. Ginsberg was unapologetic, irreverent of power structures, and reminded readers of Whitman's dream of a more open America. In his essay "The Jew as an American Poet," Allen Grossman sums up Ginsberg's situation:

> Ginsberg's poetry belongs to that strange and almost posthumous poetic literature which began to be produced in America after World War II, and in which the greatest figure is the spoiled Calvinist (Catholic), Robert Lowell. The characteristic literary posture of the postwar poet in America is that of the survivor – a man who is not quite certain that he is not in fact dead. It is here that the Jew as a symbolic figure takes on his true centrality. The position can be stated hypothetically from the point of view of a European survivor who has made the Stygian crossing to America: 'Since so many like died, and since my survival is an unaccountable accident, how can I be certain that I did not myself die and that America is not in fact Hell, as indeed all the social critics say it is?' Ginsberg's poetry is the poetry of a terminal cultural situation. It is a Jewish poetry because the Jew is the prime symbolic representative of a man overthrown by history (Poetry of Ginsberg 103).

Where Ginsberg finds success in my opinion and influences many more people than those who read poetry (though "Howl" certainly is a part) is the performance of his life. Ginsberg recognized that "silence and secrecy are the shelter of power." (Foucault 101) It is in the poem's and Ginsberg's acting out, the lack of decorum in life (and art) that creates "a stumbling block, a point of resistance and a starting point for an opposing strategy" that with a few other brave and vocal provocateurs created a counter-culture. (Foucault 101) One thinks of fellow spokes people of the day such as Abby Hoffman and Jerry Rubin. In fact, it is the poem's repeated speech act "I am with you in Rockland" that is the leaping off point to his life's work and persona after "Howl" until he was in his sixties, and after Reagan and Thatcher seemed to have the last word, TINA.

## WORKS CITED

Austin, JL. *How to Do Things with Words*. Cambridge: Harvard University Press. 1962.

Breslin, James. "The Origins of 'Howl' and 'Kaddish.'" *On the Poetry of Allen Ginsberg*. Ed. Hyde, Lewis. Ann Arbor: University of Michigan Press. 1984.

Coleridge, Samuel Taylor. *The Portable Coleridge*. The Viking Portable Library. New York: Penguin Books. 1950.

Elman, Richard. "Beyond Self-Absorption." *On the Poetry of Allen Ginsberg*. Ed. Hyde, Lewis. Ann Arbor: University of Michigan Press. 1984.

Foucault, Michel. *History of Sexuality*. Translated by. Robert Hurley. London: Penguin Books. 1990.

Gates, David. "Welcoming 'Howl' into the Canon." *The Poem that Changed America: "Howl" Fifty Years Later*. Ed. Jason Shinder. New York: Farrar, Straus, Giroux, 2006.

Ginsberg, Allen. *Howl and other Poems*. Pocket Poets, No. 4. San Francisco: City Lights, 1956.

Hoffman, Erving. *The Presentation of Self in Everyday Life*. Garden City: Doubleday Anchor Books, 1959.

Merrill, F. Thomas. *Allen Ginsberg*. Boston: Twayne Publishers, 1988.

Monteagudo, Jesse. "Allen Ginsberg." *Gay Today*. (Oct. 27, 1997). http://gaytoday.badpuppy.com/garchive/viewpoint/102797vi.htm.

Perloff, Marjorie. "A Lost Battalion of Platonic Conversationalists: 'Howl' and the Language of Modernism." *The Poem that Changed America: "Howl" Fifty Years Later*. Ed. Jason Shinder. New York: Farrar, Straus, Giroux, 2006.

Pottier, Eugene. "The Internationale." 1871. https://www.youtube.com/watch?v=VEH2jRYusrE.

Preminger, Alex & Brogan, T.V.F. *The New Princeton Encyclopedia of Poetry and Poetics*. New York: MJF Books, 1993.

Raskin, Jonah. *American Scream*. Berkeley: University of California Press, 1997.

Rosenthal, M. L. "Poet of New Violence." *On the Poetry of Allen Ginsberg*. Ann Arbor: University. of Michigan Press, 1984.

———. "The Refusal to Repress." *On the Poetry of Allen Ginsberg*. Ann Arbor: University of Michigan Press, 1984.

Tytell, John. "The Legacy of Surrealism." *On the Poetry of Allen Ginsberg*. Ann Arbor: University. of Michigan Press, 1984.

Chapter 6

## McLuhan's Warning, Frye's Strategy, Emerson's Dream

I will be referring to poetry in this essay. However, all literary writing (whether fiction, creative nonfiction, poetry, or writing about literature) practices the same associative and inductive reasoning skills. Literary writing gives students practice using associative and inductive thinking skills necessary for creative lives. I wish to help bolster the legitimacy of poetry and other forms of literary writing in academic and nonacademic cultures by calling attention to how they are tools for citizenry.

Though in "The Poet" Ralph Waldo Emerson calls out for the first American poet, he also sets the bar for the citizenry suggesting that the impressions of nature on all citizens should make them artists: "Every touch should thrill. Every man should be so much an artist that he could report in conversation what had befallen him" (249). Here and elsewhere in his essay, Emerson is suggesting that in a democracy everyone could be, should be, a poet. I think that he would even have been satisfied with each citizen being "of subtle mind, whose head appeared to be a music-box of delicate tunes and rhythms, and whose skill, and command of language, we could not sufficiently praise" (250). Given his numerous essays that call the American citizen to the poetic task, I believe that he hoped that someday every citizen in a democracy would have enough of a "subtle mind" to recognize and remember that he or she mediates his or her reality. He wished for each citizen to be a "contemporary" poet, to remember to always be open to the awe of living life, and open to the sensibility of a poet. From his first essay, Emerson tells us this. In "Nature" he states that it is up to every man to find his own truth. In fact, the essay is a call to Americans to do just that, find America's own truth as a nation:

> We must trust the perfection of the creation so far, as to believe that whatever curiosity the order of things has awakened in our minds, the order of things can satisfy. Every man's condition is a solution in hieroglyphic to those inquiries he would put. He acts it as life, before he apprehends it as truth. In like manner, nature is already, in its forms and tendencies, describing its own design. Let us interrogate the great apparition, that shines so peacefully around us. Let us inquire, to what end is nature?

That dream of citizen-poets has been lost to American society.

Joseph Brodsky calls attention to the ever growing divide between poet and citizen when he reminds society of its responsibility:

> the social function of a poet is writing, which he does not by society's appointment but by his own volition. His only duty is to his language, that is, to write well. By writing, especially by writing well, in the language of his society, a poet takes a large step toward it. It is society's job to meet him halfway, that is, to open his society, a poet takes a large step toward it. It is society's job to meet him halfway, that is, to open his book and to read it. (Stephenson)

He takes for granted the gap between reader and writer, and the "duty" and "job" recall labor instead of the sense of play found in literary writing. In fact, there seems to be something desperate in Brodsky's placing responsibilities. American culture seems to have come to validate Marshall McLuhan's speculation that it fosters "a conspiracy to make the artist a frill, a fribble, or a Milltown" (66). I don't believe the literary arts or any other art form was ever popular in the United States. However, I am attempting to affix to literary writing greater value than it has had, even in the academy.

The divide in book culture between literary writer and reader is assumed and supported in the academy. In *Differentials,* Marjorie Perloff also assumes that there has been a decline in the arts and humanities and attributes the problem at least partially to curriculum changes over the past few decades: "without clear cut notions of *why* it is worthwhile to read literary texts, whether by established or marginalized writers, in the first place, the study of 'literature' becomes no more than a chore, a way of satisfying distribution requirements" (15). Perloff urges a change in pedagogy in literary studies. She suggests, "What is urgently needed ... is a more 'differential' and inductive approach to literary study, indeed to the humanities in general" (16). Though I think the problem for the arts and humanities is one that has its roots deeper in our history, I agree with her thesis in its focus. However, I am interested in *"why* it is worthwhile" and how a teacher of literary writing brings about its value to students so that its legitimacy may be secured.

McLuhan had insight into the predicaments of the artist and audience (literary writer and reader). He rightly defined the artist broadly: "The artist is the man [sic] in any field, scientific or humanistic, who grasps the implications of his actions and of new knowledge in his own time. He is the man of integral awareness" (65). His definition is in keeping with Emerson's poet as the man who "announces that which no man foretold...the true and only doctor" and fine tunes Northrop Frye's notion that the poet doesn't make any particular or specific statements (63). He or she tells us not what happened, but what usually happens. While Aristotle refers to the difference between fact and that of universal truth, McLuhan suggests that the poet perceives new patterns of understanding. Neil Postman, one such "artist," refers to the arrival of 'new knowledge' as "great media-metaphor shift[s]" (16). These new patterns that at first disturb older patterns of understanding become conventions that are lived by.

McLuhan assumes there is much one can do about those social mythologies. Later in his book, McLuhan argues the value of the artist as the "man of integral awareness" (65). He says, "The artist can correct the sense of ratios before the blow of new technology has numbed and subliminal groping and reaction begin," and adds, "in experimental art, men are given the exact specifications of coming violence to their own psyches from their own counter-irritants or technology" (65). McLuhan is referring to the process of the creative act that allows the artist to stand outside the conventions that engage the rest of the society. The attributes he gives the artist are those of knowing how to live among old, new, and future conventions, using the attributes to think outside conventions' boxes whether they be social or academic, using the conventions to create his or her life. He writes, "The ability of the artist to sidestep the bully blow of new technology of any age, and to parry such violence with full awareness, is age old" (65). McLuhan suggests that all creative people have this ability which allows them to avoid becoming irrelevant by new technology or 19st in it.

He goes on to state that artists have the "exact information of how to rearrange one's psyche in order to anticipate the next blow from our own extended faculties" (66). McLuhan is explaining the functioning imagination and its ability to anticipate change and wonders "if men were able to be convinced that art is precise advance knowledge of how to cope with the psychic and social consequences of the next technology, would they ail become artists? Or would they begin a careful translation of new art forms into social navigation charts?" (66). Teachers whose lives involve the arts can use McLuhan's remarkable insights to their advantage because he adds legitimacy to their work. However, to use his insights to validate poetry, teachers need first to recognize it and then to call students' attention to it. They need to allow students to discover ways into art. Teachers who teach poetry writing will find Frye a good guide to this end.

By explaining literary writing, Frye moves us beyond McLuhan's implicit goals to practical strategies. In *The Educated Imagination,* Frye reinforces McLuhan and Emerson. He states, "The literary writer isn't giving information, either about a subject or about his [sic] state of mind: he's trying to let something take on its own form, whether it's a poem or play or novel or whatever…The writer of literature can only write what takes shape in his mind" (46). Frye is explaining the concentration that allows form and content or that allows content to determine the form of the student's writing.

For writers to concentrate on the shape of a piece of literature, they will need to put aesthetic distance between themselves and the conventions about which they wish to write. Once aesthetic distance is achieved, they may also achieve integral awareness or the ability to recognize the possible contexts for the conventions that they will be using. The awareness allows writers to live and work outside, among but not within conventions, or at least not immersed in the conventions upon which writers wish to concentrate. By working outside conventions, writers control their use, which ones are used and to what extent. This effort creates new *possible* conventions, from which derives the cry "make it new." Integral awareness becomes an experience of the sublime when writers, working among the conventions, recognize that the only conventions they have are the ones they make. Student writers will soon want to learn how to use references to the sublime in their writing. Presenting the unpresentable in poetry is the distance a poet travels within a poem.

I explain how to live among conventions with integral awareness to students using my version of *Alice in Wonderland*. When Alice is very small, she is a mouse in the house, lost in the convention of home or perhaps marriage. McLuhan and Quentin Fiore put it this way: "One thing about which fish know exactly nothing is water, since they have no anti-environment which would enable them to perceive the element they live in" (175). My Alice is unaware of the water, that she is McLuhan's fish. When Alice is larger than the house and wears the house as a garment, her head out a chimney, her arms out windows, the house's peak rests along her shoulders as though it were a dress, and, her legs through the house's floor, Alice is using the convention of home or marriage as a tool. She is well aware of her environment and is making it her own. The difference is one of control and lack of control of those conventions. In a world where new knowledge creates the crisis of the day, students need to learn how to use old conventions as tools so that the crisis of tomorrow doesn't overwhelm them but rather is anticipated. After all, from the crises of the day come the conventions of tomorrow.

Once students understand how to give shape on the page to what takes shape in their minds, the teacher of poetry or other literary writing then focuses students on bringing each of what Frye calls the two dreams of literature (wish fulfillment and anxiety) into conscious visions and letting their ideas take shape on paper. By helping students focus in this way, the teachers invite students to experience McLuhan's integral awareness in multiple ways. Students also begin to obtain a sense for the exact proportions necessary to prepare their psyches and prevent their reacting to each new knowledge and their own extended faculties. Student writers get this practice first by writing each kind of dream and integrating it in their writing of one work. The practice allows students to imagine how the next blow or paradigm shift might impact their worlds and how to adjust successfully to maintain their lives as creative project. Living among and not in conventions is what should be expected of an educated person.

When students take time to explore metaphor, they are given permission to resist the coercive cultural performative impulses while concentrating on allowing their topic (in relation to the context to the world around it) to take on its shape in their minds. When students work with metaphor, they begin exploring and inhabiting other worlds, other possible worlds whether those worlds are anxiety ridden or ideal or somewhere in between. What students discover is that this exercise is play and that the play of childhood is not alien to the adult world; in fact, it's integral to it. Play becomes their work, and work becomes play in that a poet takes words seriously to have fun with them. The development of the imagination isn't simply for children. Once the ambiguity of possibilities is arrived at in writing, students may also be led by language play to choose or create career paths and lifestyles that resist coercion, intimidation, and alienation.

Instructors who move beyond metaphor do students the greatest service by also introducing them to postmodern poetics, and they will continue to find Emerson a guide. When students understand Emerson's poet as "namer" ("Poet" 249) and recognize that "we live amid surfaces, and the true art of life is to skate well on them. Under the oldest mouldiest conventions a man of native force prospers just as well as in the newest world, and that by skill of handling and treatment" (275), they become empowered and may begin to understand what Ferdinand de Saussure meant by signifiers. They realize that art may be created to illustrate the alternative possible conventions to those provided them through social "reality." Students are empowered to create their own poetry and reality for themselves. When we take the idea of naming seriously, we move beyond symbolism into the world's mystery that we have been a part of all along, or, as Wallace Stevens instructs, "Phoebus was! A name for something that never could be named" (381). Now, to use words to communicate in a world without names, the writer must abandon the names of the English language and create temporary names for the subjects and objects around them. The empowerment of naming when composing a poem aids students because they are composing their own reality.

In *The Poetics of Transition,* Jonathan Levin illuminates the linkage between Emerson and postmodern poetics. He explains the imagination's function in "naming" or what he calls the aesthetics of pragmatism as follows: "The pragmatist imagination is the site where this reincorporation is endlessly negotiated. For the pragmatist, imagination is exercised in full awareness of its limitations. Pragmatists posit the ultimate value of imaginative activity even as they underscore the inadequacy of any metaphor or narrative that activity might produce" (196).

The practice of a "poetics of transition" brings students into the world of wonder that is the one they inhabit. It allows them to remind their readers of the sublime that is with them always. The pragmatist imagination is one integrally aware. Students also then create their own conventions by picking and choosing among the various parts of them. When writing poetry using symbolism, writers take it as far as the metaphysics of creation mythology. When writing postmodern poetry, writers take it to the more epistemologically honest edge of knowledge and conventions where they might find the "un presentable" sublime, the experience of being alive. The creative experience of the postmodern writer is sublime because of the terror of no logos and because of the possible worlds this allows the writer to suggest. The experience is one of Nietzsche's cosmic dancer turning work into child's play and of Sartre's "condemned to freedom." It is also Jacques Derrida's aporia, McLuhan's integral awareness, as well as Emerson's skater confronting the surfaces of things.

The benefits of students writing a postsymbolist poetry using a "poetic of transition" are clear. Not only do students write poetry that confronts the conventional names of things and avoids symbolism which requires interpretation fixed by culture, but they also learn more easily the relation between art and their lives. The idea of the sublime becomes accessible in each of their realities day to day because the students must consider the conventions before treating the subjects and objects they are writing about. The writing is more genuine. It becomes experiential. The writer and reader may come away with the experience of being alive. Each line of poetry reminds the reader and the writer of the limitations of language-the limitations of convention-and points to the sublime and fulfill Emerson's dream. What better mission for a democracy?

Mark Federman, Chief Strategist at the McLuhan Program in Culture and Technology at the University of Toronto, may help clarify the experiential nature of literary writing to students and may clarify how the practice resembles the students' world. In "The Cultural Paradox of the Global Village," in referring to contemporary art, he explains:

> It is experiential, as opposed to prescribed, pre-scripted and doctrinaire in its constructive chaos. Previously, physical objects in relation to local geography allowed us to determine much about identity. Now, in an age of instantaneous communications that eliminates the effects of geographical distance and time zones, identity is oriented by means of "scapes" that juxtapose multiple diverse environments from around the world. Thus the future, especially for emerging societies, is always elsewhere, constantly in flux, formed according to relational, as opposed to regional, patterns. Transnational traffic of ideas and experiences that are now abstract, form a new order that is ironically and paradoxically unstable, irregular, incomplete and undefined relative to our historical and physical experience. This is the new norm to which we are slowly becoming socialized. It is "broken" in our conventional sense, but that is its virtue in the reformation of a global society. In this case, the state of being broken is not a destructive force but a liberating one. As McLuhan said: "Breakdown is breakthrough."

In his explanation, Federman articulates the correlation between the world within which the writer writes and the kind of writing students would be attempting. The writing responds to the postmodern world, preparing writers for the kind of thinking they will need to do today and tomorrow. By implementing educational strategies for a postsymbolist literary writing, instructors are giving students the courage to create their own lives. By augmenting the value of literary writing throughout the educational system, we also heed McLuhan's warning, practice Frye's implicit strategy.

As a professor teaching literary writing at a small liberal arts college that is becoming more and more practical, more and more vocational, I see my job as becoming more and more difficult and more and more important. I am "the little old man who provides the adventurer with amulets against the dragon forces he[sic] is about to pass" (Campbell 69). As in the Joseph Campbell's chapter "Supernatural Aid" in *The Hero with a Thousand Faces*, I dispense a possible antidote to the wasteland that students will engage upon leaving college (69). I am comfortable with my efforts with those students whose concentration is Writing and Literature. However, the prognosis for general education students attending a class of literature or a class of literary writing seems poor to me. I doubt whether any of them have been able to use the medicines of aporia to create their own lives. I don't know whether the vaccines have inoculated anyone from the mass media world of advertisement. I do know that many of our students who are Writing and Literature concentrators and general education students from other majors long to fill job openings in the marketing career path, so the chances of any of these graduates deliberately creating their own lives looks dismal from this vantage point. I cannot report that a cadre of students is out there reshaping the world in their images. I've been teaching twenty years.

Instead, I continue to loaf and invite my students "to lean and loafe at [their] ease and observe a spear of summer grass" (Whitman 63.) For many students this will be the last time they will have the opportunity to resist the coercive social forces of convention that motivate them to be useful in established ways. For others, they will return at forty on Sunday afternoons after cutting suburban lawns to enrich sick souls with efforts in writing, a brave gesture against the overlapping conventions imprisoning them. Perhaps when my beard is whiter, I will learn of a former student or two who wrestled the dragon forces of the mundane death march to create an original life. Perhaps writing would no longer have had anything to do with that life. That would be fine. That would be a start, a citizen making a stand in integral awareness to become the poet of his or her life. Emerson would love it.

## WORKS CITED

Campbell, Joseph. *The Hero With a Thousand Faces*. Princeton: Princeton/Bollingen Series, 1968.

Emerson, Ralph Waldo. "The Poet." *Emerson: Essays and Journals*. Garden City: International Collectors Library, 1968. 247-67.

———— "Nature." https://archive.vcu.edu/english/engweb/transcendentalism/authors/emerson/nature.html.

Federman, Mark. "The Cultural Paradox of the Global Village." The McLuhan Program in Culture and Technology, 2006.
http://individual..utoronto.ca/markfederman/CulturalPilradoxOfTheGlobalVillage.pdf.

Frye, Northrop. *The Educated Imagination*. Bloomington: Indiana University Press, 1964.

Levin, Jonathan. *The Poetics of Transition*. Durham: Duke University Press, 1999.

McLuhan, Marshall. *Understanding Media: The Extensions of Man*. New York: Signet, 1964.

———— Fiore, Questin. *War and Peace in the Global Village*. New York: Bantam, 1968.

Perloff, Marjorie. *Differentials: Poetry, Poetics, Pedagogy*. Tuscaloosa: The University of Alabama Press, 2004.

Postman, Neil. *Amusing Ourselves to Death*. New York: Penguin Books, 1986.

Rorty, Richard. *Objectivity, Relativism, and Truth*. Cambridge: Cambridge University Press, 1991. p. 39.

Stephenson, Wen. "The Matter of Poetry." *The Atlantic*. May 1991.
www.theatlantic.comlunbound/poetry/poetint.htm.

Stevens, Wallace. "Notes Toward a Supreme Fiction." *The Collected Poems of Wallace Stevens*. New York: Alfred Knopf, 1978.

Thoreau, Henry David. "Economy." *Walden*. Gutenbberg.org/files/205/205-h/205-h.htm.

Welch, Lew. "Manifesto: Bread vs. Mozart's Watch." *How I Work As a Poet*. Berkeley: Grey Fox Press, 1973. p.3.

Whitman, Walt. "Song of Myself."*Collected Works of Walt Whitman*. New York: Penguin. 1962.

CHAPTER 7

## Poetry's Evolving Ecology: Toward a Post-Symbol Landscape

> "Our language and our culture are as much a contingency, as much a result of thousands of small mutations finding niches (and millions of others finding no niches), as are the orchids and anthropoids."
> (Richard Rorty, 1989)

In the town of Marblehead, Massachusetts, as in many New England coastal communities in the 21st century, homes dot the tops of tree-dominated hills with cliffs that spill into a harbor. These homes in New England often have very large double-pane windows that look out into the branches of evergreens, maples, birches, and oaks that are homes to a magnificent variety of birds. The woods that surround these homes sustain fox, rabbit, raccoons, and rumored deer and other regional wildlife. Residents and local officials are sensitive to their daily influences on the historic nature of this area and on the eco-system that makes up the region's earth, sea, and sky. Local inhabitants understand that the eco-systems are always in flux and that our presence influences that flux.

While the people who live here are at home in these houses, they are also at home in language. Their imaginations are the nimble places of possibility that allow them to articulate, influence, and perhaps survive their current evolving ecology in language and in their neighborhoods. Just as the automobiles and buildings have an impact on the ecology around houses, cultural symbols influence the ecology of language. The following reflection reviews contemporary thinking on mediation, outlines the function of the symbol from Modernism to Postmodernism, and asserts that poetry's formative imagination in Postmodernism may itself be seen as an evolutionary mechanism for marking time in contingency and as the place of possibility, allowing a world literature, culture, and perhaps language to emerge.

In his book *The Marginalization of Poetry*, Bob Perelman assumes that the absolute contact with nature, often attributed to other animals, is lost on humans and is not attainable. He does so as he reviews language poets' attempt at progress toward it. He frustrates the notion of a forward trajectory and progress in poetry. However he leaves the door open to poetry's evolution. He tells the reader, "The administered dioramas of literary history contain scenes that on a gross scale can be read clearly enough so that we can watch revolutionaries battling conservatives and fighting against genres and the genres themselves flourishing, fading, and mutating" (38-57). Terry Eagleton uses the "crude fabular form" of biblical genesis to explain how human shave moved away from a more immediate world and culture of nature's absolute; in *The Ideology of the Aesthetic*, he suggests how poets might regain paradisiacal relevance. Both of these authors address the growing irrelevance of poetry to all citizens. According to Eagleton, people conventionalize mediation, including their alienation, embracing what he calls a "dissociation of sensibilities' in politics, ethics, and aesthetics" (366-415).

Marjorie Perloff, in her essay "On Steve McCaffrey's 'Lag,'" recognizes a dialectic between popular culture and poetry as worth watching during the "evolution" of the twentieth-century poetic, when she writes about McCaffrey's Black Debt (114). The deteriorating situation between poetry and any audience marks a continuation of the crisis in the humanities that postmodern theorists argue began with the Enlightenment. The idea of evolution—whether it means change or progress toward an unmediated poetry—is an often disputed idea in the arts; yet an unmediated poetry may be the only way to attract a larger audience in late capitalism. The scientific language used by these authors in their discussion of poetry is not new to it. Indeed, evolution may be helpful as a loose metaphor to explain the effects of globalization and of multiculturalism on the formative imagination of the poet, and thus to decipher how that imagination may help shape the idea of world literature. If "evolution" is a helpful term, then using the idea that poetry's ecology is the result of formative imagination at work may also be helpful.

The poet Stephen Spender defines the formative imagination as the ever-metamorphosing imagination responding to contingency as it builds or deconstructs its world through the language the poet uses. In two lectures for Audio-Forum, Sound Seminars in the last century, Stephen Spender tracked the origins of what is today meant by contingency. One is titled, "Necessity of Being Absolutely Modern" and the second is "Poetic Vision and Modern Literature." In the title of the first lecture, Spender is referring to Arthur Rimbaud's genius as one believing in the magic of language. Spender recounts his having lived the Modernist movement from beginning to end in a span of two years. In the second lecture, he explains the inverted nature of visionary writing by modern poets and novelists. For poets such as Blake, New Jerusalems are described in full. For modern poets, they are alternative values referred to or gestured toward merely. There too he comes back to magic: not the magic of language only, but a magic of cultural creation mythology (Absolutely Modern). The magic acts of Modernism seem to have been an attempt through therapy to heal what Paul Valéry called "the disorder of mind" in the mind of Europe (Valéry 96).

In the first lecture, Spender refers to a "melting back of the formative imagination" as the magic of poetry working to re-create reality and to cure the early twentieth-century affliction. He uses this idea convincingly to illustrate Rimbaud's disillusionment with modern poetry (Absolutely Modern). The same issue seems to have plagued modern poets: literary legend has it that Ezra Pound insisted from a cage in Italy that he speak with Churchill, Stalin, and Roosevelt. Pound believed that with the right combination of words, he could convince them that they were on the wrong side in the war. Spender suggests that modern poets believed that the melting back of the formative imagination to the creation myth of Western culture would allow them to start again, fresh in Eden, I presume, perhaps from the moment before the fall; this time correcting mistakes and doing it right (Absolutely Modern).

In his second lecture on visionary Modernism, Spender explains how the utopian impulses of modern literature thrash around the suffering of the artist who is stuck with aristocratic sympathies and the fading of Christianity in an ever shrinking or globalizing and industrialized world. He concludes the lecture with the idea that the impetus of a movement beginning with Baudelaire has changed and that "the main spring" of the impetus has been removed (Poetic Vision). He suggests to the reader that the main spring is the artist's cultural search for a pathway back to some mythic utopian Judeo-Christian cultural beginning. The Holocaust and the intermingling of cultures via political and economic imperialism, or through other desperate and democratic motives, removed from Modernism the metaphor of the "main spring" of cultural creation mythologies (Poetic Vision). Language's contingency, caused by the aporia between signified and signifier, has replaced it, thus Perelman's assumption. Language's contingency applies to all languages and so contains a broader appeal for poetry of all cultures. The magic may now be in the naming, the wall against which poets beat their heads.

The formative imagination is important because it implies that impress or evolutionary inheritance may be malleable, sensitive to its environment, to its ecology. Just as the stem cell can produce any cell, the formative imagination is an active agent and it promises to transform impress through the contingency of postmodern/post-avant poetry. However, instead of melting the imagination back to Eden, formative imagination may itself be seen as an evolutionary mechanism marking time in contingency, the place of possibility, allowing a world literature, culture, and perhaps language to emerge. The national impresses of languages, nationalism, and religion may prevent a world culture, literature, and language from forming. However, as with species of plants and animals, the world is losing languages all the time in the postmodern world. If we look at the development of language and literature in the once colonial America and at the struggle of Modernism in the West, we might infer how on a larger scale world literature may evolve.

The war between Modernists like Eliot and Williams may have been inspired by petty jealousies on perhaps both sides, but it is the crossroads. The struggle of Modernism may be seen as one of direction by Western nationalism and its cultures in response to Valéry's psychological diagnosis. If so, then Eliot's and Pound's guarding as gatekeepers of Western and national histories and high cultures was one direction. Another was suggested by Williams' iconoclastic exhortation:

> It's the words, the words we need to get back to, words washed clean. [...] Stein has gone systematically to work smashing every connotation that words have ever had, in order to get them back clean. [...] It can't be helped that the whole house has to come down. In fact the whole house has to come down. [...]. And it's got to come down because it has to be rebuilt. And it has to be rebuilt by unbound thinking. (163)

Though Wallace Stevens' poetry may have been more successful with Williams' aim, Williams' articulation was to point the direction of art and culture upon the victory of the allies in World War II. Of course, at the time, the implications of the victory to culture and nationalism were not obvious, any more than the victories of capitalism and democracy were obvious.

In the West (Western Europe and the Western Hemisphere), the victory of the allies was going to mean movement toward capitalism and democracy as though they were one. It meant an unspoken promise to open global cultural gates so that the "barbarians" (local under-served, subaltern, and "other" cultural populations alike), could perhaps take part, even if illiterate, in poverty, and on the margins. The contingency implied in the movement mentioned above might be thought of as evolutionary in nature. For many countries capitalism entered via the wooden horse of democracy. Of course, half the world remained under communist influence, including places close to American soil, such as Cuba. (In fact, Cuba didn't become communist until a decade after the WW II.) For democracy to take place in the West (including what remained to be achieved in the USA), the cultural symbols had to begin to fall away. Structuralists saw this happening and many dislike the developments in the contemporary world that have caused cultures to lose their identities. Shedding cultural symbols was easy in the United States, where the impress of Britain could easily be denied and where artists such as Williams and Stevens were attempting to create an American literature. In fact, Northrop Frye went so far as to say that the USA may have indeed created its own literature (43-44). Though it has been argued that the world is being Americanized, that is not so if one means a culture adopting American or Western symbols. What is Western is the lack of permanent metaphors or concrete symbols. The West has come to embrace change only.

In Europe, identity had expressed itself in distinct, individual symbols for centuries, and not simply for and by the elite, though most forcefully by them for sure. To some both inside and outside it, the European Union today may appear to be a stew of symbols. The significance of poets and populations responding to this circumstance is their questioning or abandoning of historical narratives and cultural symbols as sacred texts, as well as their embracing—or at least acknowledging—the function of the formative imagination as the adapter for or as the threshold to contingency. The shedding of cultural symbols in Europe appears to be both difficult and yet urgent. Immigrant and indigenous peoples feel their core cultural values—ones that symbols represent—threatened. This includes the values within the current zeitgeists of each group. Immigrant populations and indigenous citizens will need to shed cultural symbols, though it may be difficult.

The response to the identity crisis in the West meant a victory for the merchant class or capitalism over the aristocracy, church, and even the state. It also meant that Modernism and its Freudian attempt at a therapeutic embracing and exploring of symbols were not going to be effective in societies and the marketplace, even with a last minute, half-hearted effort to educate the masses. Capitalism and technology brought the need for perpetual social change. When global society's experience is continuous change, history and symbols do not address the experience. Myth does not have time to form. When a society respects change as its paradigm, it must embrace chance, contingency. Tradition no longer projects the illusion of holding time still; nor do totems, creation myths, or symbols suffice to describe shared experience. In fact, shared experience is fractured. Only metaphor and irony address society with a nimbleness worthy of chance and rapid change, not necessarily with therapeutic intentions, but with an ability to manage that experience, or perhaps create new descriptions of it.

Richard Rorty tells us that the only effective philosophical way of addressing our situation is "to redescribe lots and lots of things in new ways, until you have created a pattern of linguistic behavior which will tempt the rising generation to adopt it, thereby causing them to look for appropriate new forms of nonlinguistic behavior [...] to drop the idea of 'intrinsic nature,' [...] to face up to the contingency of the language we use" (Rorty 9). Here he brings change and chance to language, recognizing its metamorphic powers, bringing Kuhn and Wittgenstein together. In doing so, he acknowledges intellectual history as the history of metaphor, an explanation unlike the one of an evolutionary biologist. However, he also goes on to explain that new epochs in art and science happen when someone notices that two descriptions conflict and then invents a replacement (12-16). Rorty implies that symbols may be used, but only when the replacement metaphor is adopted by society.

I am suggesting that we may be in an epoch of Western languages redescribing via paralogy, using new images and metaphors in an attempt to find perhaps—and only perhaps—replacement symbols, or to rid the world of metaphysics and foster the embracing of contingency. Due to capitalism and its offshoots of globalization and multiculturalism, symbols will not hold for any culture. The period known as postmodern, if described in Darwinian language, may be a generation producing many mutations into its cultural ecology, many metaphors, and may continue until there is a world literature that fills the definition that Goethe famously left blank. This idea runs counter to the view of the left that sees globalization as a kind of social Darwinism. Though my sympathies are there, the West's momentum is not abating, even during major economic troubles. With the continued loss of languages, the adoption of English for business, and the lack of a counter-weight against globalization, I see the possibility eventually of one tongue. That language might be called English, but I would bet that we would not recognize it just as we have trouble recognizing Old or even Middle English. I have chosen poems from two poets all the rage in America, if "all the rage" might continue to be applied to poetry: Jorie Graham and Charles Bernstein. The poems that I was able to access via the internet are "Prayer" and "In Particular." The first poem is a redescription of religious and cultural symbols. It attempts to explain a daily religious ritual in Darwinian terms. And the second is an attempt to abandon cultural symbols and metaphors of any kind.

Jorie Graham's poem "Prayer" offers an example of poetry's evolving away from religious symbols. The poem seems to be apologizing for religious symbols, given that the fish possesses symbolic value as well in Christianity as in Darwinian thought. The symbol is pivotal, moving from religious metaphysics to Enlightenment. Though the poem uses the prayer as a symbol for culture, it attempts to explain the gesture as no more than a cultural unifier and as futile in the light of evolution. The poem uses fish, minnows' coordinated yet ineffective movements in water, as metaphors for human prayer to illustrate how the current, a pun here, moves the fish in directions they do not necessarily want to go. They cannot create the current; however, they are changed by it. The speaker expresses faith in the fact that they will all move together and be changed together:

> [...] [...] without the way to create current, making of their unison (turning, reinfolding, entering and exiting their own unison in unison) making of themselves a visual current, one that cannot freight or sway by minutest fractions the water's downdrafts and upswirls, [...][...] (Poets.Org)

By putting humans with the rest of the animal kingdom, Graham is transforming the great symbols of Christian religion and its cultures that had placed humans closer to God. Metaphor and irony are her tools. God as spotlight on humans is not mentioned, nor are there humans in the poem, except for the narrator. The minnows function as metaphors for all of us.

> [...][...] a real current though mostly invisible sending into the visible (minnows) arrowing motion that forces change—this is freedom. This is the force of faith. Nobody gets what they want. Never again are you the same. The longing is to be pure. What you get is to be changed. [...][...] (Poets.Org)

Here Graham highlights the psychology of religions in a manner that is almost Nietzschean in its implications. In the will to power, all the horde gets is the will but not the power. What the horde or the slaves to religions get is "to be changed," but changed together one assumes. The narrator of the poem also tells us:

> [...]I cannot of course come back. Not to this. Never. It is a ghost posed on my lips. Here: never. (Poets.Org)

The narrator and the fish must move with the current and are changed; never able to be whom they were before. Even the way in which the words are typed out in the last sentence of the poem tells the reader how (s)he forced to move on, even against the strength of the colon: "Here: never."

The shift from religious symbolism to Enlightenment symbols and metaphors moves a faith in the miracle that a school of minnows will stir their own current into minnow current events. The shift is one toward recognition of contingency and despair, with no hope except for the cultural change that unity, communion brings the school. We learn by one more poet that the dead science of religion has been subsumed by the language of physical science. We learn that the poet is one bridging religious faith to the Enlightenment, not a terribly revolutionary task, but one illustrative of my point. We learn the divide between the frontier of sciences and the domain of logic. The poem does not further assist evolution towards contemporary secular culture. Nor does it explain the movement from religious cultural symbols to the postmodern world via sciences and the Enlightenment.

There are many examples of post-symbol poems, especially among the younger generation. However, examples of playful mediation and of the removal of cultural symbols can more particularly be found in Charles Bernstein's poetry. His poem "In Particular," published online in *Jacket* Magazine, attempts to envelop the globe as well as to remain local and particular to his style of post-symbol poetry. The poem resists stereotypes but keeps a pedestrian tone to its list form conceit. It tempts the reader at least as much as Williams' poetry did with its relying so heavily on a red wheelbarrow beside white chickens. The title itself boldly points the reader away from the idea of symbol and metaphor. However, the reader's imagination will compose metaphors with little help. The reader is confronted with a list of what seems to be particular examples of what we do not know because the sentences appear to be incomplete fragments. The list of people along with their objects lacks verbs that could create metaphors. It begins giving the reader multicultural understanding:

> A black man waiting at a bus stop
> A white woman sitting on a stool
> A Philippino eating a potato
> A Mexican boy putting on shoes
> [...](Jacket 19)

Not until the reader gets to "A Hindu hiding in Igloo/" does (s)he question the list of particulars. At this point, the reader is moved from the outside world of what might have been a 360-degrees or global description in a particular spot to the poet's inner environment. It is at this point that the poet begins the joy of his dance through aporia after aporia: "A Christian lady with toupee/[...]/A barbarian with beret/[...]/A Beatnik writing a limerick/[...]/An Armenian rowing to Amenia/[...]/A Mongolian imitating Napoleon/[...]" (Jacket 19), and so on until he sets the reader back down:

> [...]
> A Mongolian chiropodist at a potluck
> A Sao Paulo poet reflecting on deflection
> A white man sitting on stool
> A black woman waiting at bus stop
> (Jacket 19)

Where a white woman and a black man begin the poem, a white man and black woman end it, replacing them. Did the narrator, after his/her dervish dance overwhelmed the reader with particulars, return to find a bus had come and gone? Or did the narrator get the gender wrong on two counts upon approaching two of his subjects? Inquiring minds want to know. Bernstein seems to know that the Earth's ecology is evolving through the growing populations who are more mobile and seems to witness the impact of their particular presences in a world of mixed cultures. His human species seem to stir their own current events for themselves, and the poem gives this impression without explicit action on the part of the humans.

The poem reminds this particular reader of one half of an André Breton list poem. By one half, I mean each line is broken, a fragment so that we get a list, but the surreal metaphor is missing. There are no verbs, simply qualified nouns, subjects of possible sentences, we may suppose. One half of the poem is particular to Bernstein's imagination and the other particular to the reader's. By constructing the poem of often unlikely particulars, Bernstein exaggerates the once-in-a-lifetime, the Now of the sublime fleeting with each itemization. The poem bridges the gulf between the dynamism of postcolonial, multicultural society, contemporary theory that embraces both deferment of judgment through aporia, and the West's value for the individual person. Graham's poem brings the reader through Modernism. Bernstein's poem, stripped as it is of cultural symbols, brings the reader into the ecology of contemporary life and poetics with its reminder that language is a medium and that the reader is expected to interact with the medium, as the reader does with his/her eco-system. Bernstein places us among the humanity in the poem in such a way that we may experience and celebrate our multicultural responsibilities as we do in the greater ecology.

One may find the shedding of cultural symbols in the development of my poetry as well. My book *Apple in the Monkey Tree* is meant to be an irreverent examination of the mixing of scientific language into the Greco-Judeo-Christian mythologies. Though a poet's discussion of intentions distracts from the reader's interactive play that the work provides, the reflective nature of this essay allows me to do so, briefly. The book's introductory poem, printed in full below, attempts to superimpose the limbs of the tree of the Old and New Testaments into the palms of Darwin's monkey, while referring to Greek mythology, Freudian ideas, and an Eastern mindset. I hoped the genius (the human monkey) would be the apple and the tree. The "Blessed metamorphosis" is supposed to be Eastern in thinking and Postmodernist in its suggestion of contingency:

**The Monkey in the Apple Tree**

Even though the genius continues
to hang on a limb and loneliness
remains a peck of liver, in the apple tree
the monkey's eyes are at last, moon and sun.
The blue ball, once a plain's guarded secret,
bounds beyond the zoo of fingertips:
The most precious desire remains to be picked,
our history, a basket of polished gourds.
The trunk from which the Bible is made
was erected by the libidos

of average television service personnel,
who crane their figures to witness space launches.
Branches that lift the cans of beer
sacrifice hair and clarity of grip
for random acts of charity
and the curiosity of human position.
Fruit and thorns will always be with us,
but now we examine the black fields of energy:
Tufts of gravity; mite-ish waves;
sacks of flesh too soon too heavy for bone.
Oh forsaken, God cants, "up your mantric spine
with conscious nests." One by one
our delusions fly away. Blessed metamorphosis
absorbs the sweat of our brows.
(The Apple in the Monkey Tree, 3)

Later poems in the book attempt to continue where the first poem leaves off. "Circus Act" (73) is one of the last poems, and it suggests that when mythological trees of the world have been climbed and imitated by humans, we can honor our animal natures and recognize the wilderness via postmodern lenses. A poem 15 to 20 years later in the development of my works perhaps an example of the fish losing its cultural significance as the poem defines poetry. The poem was written as an interactive nature poem where the poet relies on signifiers and aporia only. It is interactive because it invites the reader to move from the restaurant seat to a plate on a table.

**Menu**

Fish hook with line cut

(Right Hand Pointing, 4)

Artists employing an interactive poetic—one that rejoins performance art with experience in visual art and poetry to form a more ecological whole—may at least bring more balance to mediation. The work being done in the sciences to understand the aporian gap between human languages and animal world may aid in eliminating mediation someday. Who knows? Slavoj Žižek, in The Indivisible Remainder, imagines quantum physics to deconstruct nature and possibly change the paradigm, if not solve the problem that mediation makes, for humans—his tongue firmly in his cheek (Žižek 218-220). Until then or until a more unified world culture perhaps, poetry's ecology is one of agility and one in flux: post-symbol. Just as the Earth's resources are being expended and its climate threatened via an economy's perpetual motion, so poetry responds and anticipates, attempting to redescribe or at least agilely aid the formative imaginations of readers. There is little time or space and little relevance for religious and cultural symbols, unless we develop global symbols, a global culture. Through capitalism's globalization much will be lost. We can only hope that other areas of diversity will find meaning. Until a global culture emerges, the signifier and the writer who reminds readers of the aporia between him/her and the signified, remain—the only useful tools of the poet, the tool also known as the gap and the tool in which possibility resides.

## WORKS CITED

Bernstein, Charles. "In Particular." *Jacket* 19 (October 2002). www.jacketmagazine.com/19/bern.html.
Eagleton, Terry. "From the Polis to Postmodernism." *The Ideology of the Aesthetic*. Cambridge: Blackwell Publishers, 1997.
Frye, Northrop. *The Educated Imagination*. Bloomington: Indiana University Press, 1964.
Graham, Jorie. "Prayer." Poets.Org. Academy of American Poets. www.poets.org/viewmedia.php/prmMID/16375.
Lawler, James and Mathews, Jackson, eds. *Paul Valéry: An Anthology*. Princeton: Princeton University Press, 1977.
Murphy, Richard. "Menu," Ed. Dale Wisely, *Right Hand Pointing* 7. www.righthandpointing.net.
———. "The Monkey in the Apple Tree" in *The Apple in the Monkey Tree*. New Paltz: Cod Hill Press, 2008.
Perelman, Bob. "Here and Now on Paper: The Avant-Garde Particulars of Robert Grenier." *The Marginalization of Poetry*. Princeton: Princeton University Press, 1996.
Perloff, Marjorie. "Signs are Taken for Wonders: On Steve McCaffrey's 'Lag.'" *Contemporary Poetry Meets Modern Theory*. Ed. Anthony Eastope and John O. Thompson. Toronto: University of Toronto Press, 1992. p. 108-115.
Rorty, Richard. *Contingency, Irony, and Solidarity*. Cambridge: Cambridge University Press, 1989.
Spender, Stephen. "Necessity of Being Absolutely Modern." Audio-Forum, Sound Seminars, 1953.
———. "Poetic Vision and Modern Literature." Audio-Forum, Sound Seminars, 1953.
———. *Journals 1939-1983*. New York: Farber and Faber, 1985.
Williams, William Carlos. *Selected Essays*. New York: New Directions Books, 1954.
Žižek, Slavoj. "Quantum Physics with Lacan." *The Indivisible Remainder: On Schelling and Related Matters*. New York: Verso Books, 2007.

CHAPTER 8

## Living Culture/Reading Poetry

> The long tradition of naivety and self-righteousness that disfigures our intellectual history, the cult of the expert is both self-serving and fraudulent…It is the responsibility of the intellectual to speak truth and expose lies.
> (Noam Chomsky, 2002)

> There are new rules: If you have money, you count—no money, you're nothing. Who cares if you've read all of Hegel? "Humanities" started sounding like a disease. "All you people are capable of is carrying around a volume of Mandelstam.
> (Svetlana Alexievich, 2016)

> [T]he social function of a poet is writing, which he does not by society's appointment but by his own volition. His only duty is to his language, that is, to write well. By writing, especially by writing well, in the language of his society, a poet takes a large step toward it. It is society's job to meet him halfway, that is, to open his book and to read it.
> (Joseph Brodsky, 1995)

We live our culture for good or ill. American culture may have had a dream of itself influenced by if not living within, a broad democratic lexicon given to it by arts and humanities. However, that dream is no longer dreamed. What colleagues in the arts and humanities call vernacular literature describes well the language that has influenced the culture in which we live, if language is the house of being (Heidegger 239). Corporate culture appropriated a naïve dream of a democratic popular culture and turned it into their pop culture using herding strategies that under-educated. Now biological, behavioral, and computer science and technology (techno-capitalists) threaten to limit subjectivity all together. The tampering with neuro-circuitry comes during a lacuna in capitalism that leaves us an opportunity for change. Let's consider some history of warnings. We live our culture for good or ill. American culture may have had a dream of itself influenced by if not living within, a broad democratic lexicon given to it by arts and humanities. However, that dream is no longer dreamed. What colleagues in the arts and humanities call vernacular literature describes well the language that has influenced the culture in which we live, if language is the house of being (Heidegger 239). Corporate culture appropriated a naïve dream of a democratic popular culture and turned it into their pop culture using herding strategies that under-educated. Now biological, behavioral, and computer science and technology (techno-capitalists) threaten to limit subjectivity all together. The tampering with neuro-circuitry comes during a lacuna in capitalism that leaves us an opportunity for change. Let's consider some history of warnings.

## History

In the 1920s and 30s, advertisements shifted from a persuasion via reason to persuasion via emotion thanks to Edward Bernays and Walter Lippmann who persuaded government and businesses to use the media to quietly rule the country. Bernays's and Lippmann's books *Propaganda* and *Public Opinion* argued that "experts" (especially the ones in advertising and public relations) are the primary agents of power. Both books explain how business and government may use experts in advertising effectively to achieve what Slavoj Žižek now calls the "dictator in democracy" (*Pervert's Guide*). Edward Bernays's 1928 book begins with the following three paragraphs.

> The conscious and intelligent manipulation of the organized habits and opinions of the masses is an important element in democratic society. Those who manipulate this unseen mechanism of society constitute an invisible government which is the true ruling power of our country.
>
> We are governed, our minds are molded, our tastes formed, our ideas suggested, largely by men we have never heard of. This is a logical result of the way in which our democratic society is organized. Vast numbers of human beings must cooperate in this manner if they are to live together as a smoothly functioning society.
>
> Our invisible governors are, in many cases, unaware of the identity of their fellow members in the inner cabinet. (37)

Here, Bernays is laying the groundwork for a smoothly functioning "democratic" society by manipulating the masses invisibly through the media. One might now be dismayed that once business schools were institutions outside university and now they run the universities. Today, marketing and business programs are taught in colleges and universities while liberal arts and art and literature programs play a small role if any. Since the Powell Memo and the Trilateral Commission's "Crisis in Democracy" in 1971 that called for moderation in democracy and accused "institutions responsible for indoctrinating the young" of not doing their jobs, the arts and humanities have declined and may soon be institutions outside the university (Chomsky, "Mainstream Media" 1:11:42).

What Bernays and Lippmann advocate is a way to seduce the masses into a happy capitalist prison where the keepers and guards are free CEOs and bankers, and the prisoners are citizen consumers who are required to be happy and "must be forced to be free" if they were ever to be offered the sobriety of freedom (Pervert's Guide). Herbert Marcuse would come to call the happy capitalist conviction "repressive desublimation." According to Marcuse's 1964 *One-Dimensional Man*, children are indoctrinated into a master/slave consumer culture where:

> [t]he means of communication, the irresistible output of the entertainment and information industry carry with them prescribed attitudes and habits, certain intellectual and emotional reactions which bind the consumers to the producers and, through the latter to the whole social system. The products indoctrinate and manipulate; they promote a false consciousness which is immune against its falsehood...Thus emerges a pattern of one-dimensional thought and behavior. (11)

He clearly articulates the ideology that is the starting point.

> We may distinguish both true and false needs. "False" are those which are superimposed upon the individual by particular social interests in his repression: the needs which perpetuate toil, aggressiveness, misery, and injustice... The result then is euphoria in unhappiness. Most of the prevailing needs to relax, to have fun, to behave and consume in accordance with the advertisements, to love and hate what others love and hate, belong to this category of false needs. (4, 5)

Theodor Adorno described the coercion of capitalist ideology this way in "Resignation:" "One should join in. Whoever only thinks, removes himself, is considered weak, cowardly, virtually a traitor" (290). Hannah Arendt's assessment is blunt: "The fundamental contradiction of the country is political freedom coupled with social slavery" (166). So much for the Enlightenment. In his book *Liquid Evil*, Zygmunt Bauman also states it clearly, "The phenomenon of 'brainwashing' is eminently present nowadays in both propaganda and commercial advertising – though hiding under the politically correct names of 'advertising,' 'broadcasting,' public relations,' downright to 'information service,' and resorting to Joseph Nye's 'soft,' instead of 'hard,' variety of power" ("Cosmopolitanism" 56:43).

In the early 1960s literary scholar and critic Northrop Frye argued that a citizen who votes must follow Adorno's implicit resistance and be "weak, cowardly, virtually a traitor" and learn how to "educate his imagination" against the "mob" and its "social illusion" fostered by advertiser and government propaganda" (14). Early in the 1960s during the second wave of mass marketing Frye warned literate people about marketing. For Harvard University's Massey Lectures Frye wrote what then was later published as a book *The Educated Imagination*. He understood how vital thinking for oneself was to democracy and wrote:

> The first thing our imaginations have to do for us, as soon as we can handle words well enough to read and write and talk, is to fight to protect us from falling into the illusions that society threatens us with. The illusion is itself produced by the social imagination, of course, but it's an inverted form of imagination. What it creates is the imaginary, which as I said earlier is different from the imaginative. (89)

Frye's fear was that of the power of the illusionary force that he called the "social imagination." He saw how the mob (now called consumers or pop culture in general) could easily fall under its power and into delusion. The struggle involved in not falling under its power is Blake's "mental fight" and Martin Heidegger's task of "shepherd of being" (252).

If not with Bernays and Lippman then in the 1960s we may begin to measure the loss of liberal arts education. It is where the ethics in marketing ends and social illusion begins. In classrooms around the USA our inability to perform Frye's method for maintaining open and independent minds doomed us to our ideology and to our lack of hope for freedom and the lack of hope for a democratic lexicon provided by the arts and humanities.

By the 80s, Neal Postman in *Amusing Ourselves to Death* could state the obvious when he remarked that maturity isn't required for our ideology and explained, "They provide a slogan, a symbol or a focus that creates for the viewers a comprehensive and compelling image of themselves." He goes on to write the following:

> By combining in compact form music, drama, imagery, humor and celebrity, the TV commercial has mounted the most serious assault on capitalist ideology since "Das Kapital" was published. To understand why, we must remember that capitalism was an outgrowth of the Enlightenment. Its theorists believed it to be based on the idea that both buyer and seller are mature, well-informed and reasonable enough to be able to engage in transactions of mutual self-interest. (126-27)

Regarding television in general, Postman explains how maturity is not a way to engage ideology:

> Television is our culture's principal mode of knowing about itself. Therefore—and this is the critical point—how television stages the world becomes the model for how the world is properly to be staged. It is not merely that on the television screen entertainment is the metaphor for all discourse. It is that off the screen the same metaphor prevails. (92)

A few pages later, Postman explains how the mode functions to re-mind the viewer, how his or her brain is programmed, altered:

> Television is altering the meaning of 'being informed' by creating a species of information that might properly be called disinformation. Disinformation does not mean false information. It means misleading information—misplaced, irrelevant, fragmented or superficial information—information that creates the illusion of knowing something, but which in fact leads one away from knowing. (107)

Perhaps by the 1980s, it was too late to save ourselves from negative effects of Bernays' negative use of empathy. We didn't believe any of the voices warning us, or we were too busy amusing ourselves to turn off screens and start thinking for ourselves and knowing the difference between envy and empathy.

In 1988, Noam Chomsky and Edward Herman also came forward with *Manufacturing Consent: The Political Economy of the Mass Media* where they explain that at that point in history "advertising that doesn't heed the model will not survive" (14-15). Herman and Chomsky make clear the mechanisms that reveal the model that the elite uses to bring into reality Bernays' strategy for making a mockery of democracy in the USA.

> A propaganda model focuses on the inequity of wealth and power and its multilevel effects on mass-media interests and choices. It traces the routes by which money and power are able to filter out the news fit to print, marginalize dissent, and allow the government and dominant private interests to get their messages across to the public. The essential ingredients of the propaganda model, or set of news "filters," fall under the following headings: 1) the size, concentrated ownership, owner wealth, and profit orientation of the dominant mass-media firms; 2) advertising as the primary income source of the mass media; 3) the reliance of the media on information provided by government, business, and "experts" funded and approved by these primary sources and agents of power; 4) "flak" as a means of disciplining the media; and 5) "anticommunism" as a national religion and control mechanism. (2)

What Herman and Chomsky are referring to is advertisements and marketing campaigns that pay for "news fit to print." The advertisements just as much (if not more) treat the viewers not as adults interested in rational thinking but children by tapping into emotions in the guise of rational thought. Furthermore, we are told in *Manufacturing Consent*, "With advertising, the free market does not yield a neutral system in which final buyer choice decides. The advertisers' choices influence media prosperity and survival" (14). We can see how the viewer is kept flowing from one program to another so that the viewer is exposed to advertisements' reassurance in television programming and how advertising that doesn't heed the model will not survive. For this same reason advertisers will not support controversial programming fearing fewer viewers however it is defined.

The arts and humanities became irrelevant when Arthur Danto could write, "[N]othing need mark the difference, outwardly, between Andy Warhol's *Brillo Box*

*Prophetic Voice Now*

and the Brillo boxes in the supermarket."(13) On this foot bridge Jean Baudrillard declared capitalist poetry the victor. Baudrillard reminds us that the disappearance of art by its minimization into mime has been going on for a century before Warhol's art. Baudrillard states, "Like all disappearing forms, art seeks to duplicate itself by means of simulation, but it will nevertheless soon be gone, leaving behind an immense museum of artificial art and abandoning the field completely to advertising."(140) ) We might also call that moment in history an intersection of appropriation, where Warhol's art is also traveling in the opposite direction to call attention to the banality-maker's power to flatten possibility into a fatal and fatalistic capitalism. Colleagues once looked down their noses and called advertisements, vernacular poetry; however, advertisements are our culture's poetry. They are the poetry with the readership that literary writers could only dream about. They also perform as the glue that holds the culture together in a way that artists and thinkers only might have hoped to. We have been warned plenty. Even as late as 1995, Nobel Laureate Joseph Brodsky published "An Immodest Proposal" where he wrote:

> The latest census that I've seen gives the population of the United States as approximately 250 million. This means that a standard commercial publishing house, printing this or that author's first or second volume, aims at only .001 percent of the entire population. To me, this is absurd...Poetry must be available to the public in far greater volume than it is. It should be as ubiquitous as the nature that surrounds us... (200-01)

## THE TWO KINDS OF POETRY

What I am calling capitalist poetry is a multi-media, mixed genre, interactive advertisement vignette performed and re-enacted. It cynically uses empathy, metaphor, irony, images, rhythm, tone, etc. to flatten and make banal. Requiring little reading and no thinking, it uses Roland Barthe's "spectacle," and its sublime exploits the consumer through fantasy and rewards financially the CEO and stockholders: Not as sublimely awe-inspiring as the Milky Way. Two examples of capitalist poetry are unpacked below.

Nike's trademark, a check mark or a lightening flash, more often than not, also carries the command "Just Do It." The three-word command (with lightning or check mark image, if one can't read those words) is stronger than a haiku (Nike). The poem may have once additionally promoted exercise, but it was also promoting, demanding thoughtlessness, obedience, impulsivity, and even compulsive behavior from the reader as it does today. The fantasy to be someone else, an envied idol distracts the reader from the struggle that is his/her life while demanding that the reader become poorer in the process: Fantasy substitutes for reality. You need these if you are going to be so-and-so.

Closets become filled with ghosts of fantasies that ended up proving to the purchaser that he/she isn't the idol after all, isn't faster after all, isn't a thinker after all, and won't be richer after all. Sweat shop poverty via cheap or slave labor and "hood" poverty give to the wealthy: Trickle up economics as usual. The sublime is for the receiver of the contents of wallets from purchases of a mass produced tease, what is known as systemic (objective) violence. The ever shrinking engagement of a person with his/her past and future that "Just Do It" suggests makes the sense of self more tenuous, breaking down identification for hypnosis and other grounds for maladies, such as consumer as slave. "Slave" leads me to my second example.

An all-American example of capitalist and racist poetry is a multi-media, mixed-genre interactive vignette performance which results in the success of the marketing for Kentucky Fried Chicken franchises. KFC advertisement vignette fantasies are filled with "micro-aggressions" if not racist assaults and induce a kind of amusement park or theme park re-enactment from the target audience (Kentucky Fried Chicken). The target-audience for marketing KFC in America has been and is the poorer African American community as an inexpensive alternative to going out to eat at a restaurant where one can't afford to eat. Southern fried was/is a way of altering the preparation of inexpensive protein that was/is often the only protein for the poor so that the mundane has flavor and perhaps hides less choice or rotting meat, perhaps deep-fried protein was the reward that came with freedom after slavery? And so the fantasy begins.

Colonel Sanders is a southern gentleman persona. His costume suggests a southern veteran of the Civil War, who continues to call himself colonel while pitching advertisements to, and feeding, poor, and largely black people, as though his property. One could argue that he is overseeing his plantation, his people. He could be a kind and beneficent owner of soup kitchens where food isn't free but fast, cheap, and makes no long-term health claims. The "meal" is brought home in a "bucket." Farm animals have eaten out of buckets, and from all accounts slaves used buckets to pick through the pile of garbage for pig intestines in the back of the Big House to supplement meager rations. The beneficent protein provider often chuckles at the viewer from the Big House, the people who fork over the cash for the pail and eat with fingers that they lick when finished. The theme park experience of the farm animal can be enjoyed by people from around the world.

The poem as advertisement is multi-media because it uses television, radio, internet, and road signs to persuade, to gain empathetic, identification responses to images of family and friends by a multinational corporation. It is interactive because of the exchange of money for an experience that is both temporarily beneficial (it fills bellies) and subconsciously humiliating, if not unhealthy in the long term. The experience is exploitation, indeed oppression, with money moving from the poor to the rich and doesn't reward the audience and re-enactor beyond the full belly. It gives the global overseas participant the American slave state experience (subconsciously if not consciously) of a plantation owner continuing to oversee his domain, his property, and the viewer and purchaser are his property; it's a Disney ride of sorts. The plantation experience continues to echo through our history providing objective violence. In fact, the latest marketing campaign for "five-dollar fill-ups" tweaks the viewers' noses as though noses were car horns connected to gas tanks.

Where a capitalist poet's empathy is a cynical experience of envy, a modern mainstream literary poet might issue an experience of the sublime by way of winning the empathy of the reader and overwhelming senses with the experience or epiphany of the persona usually at the end of the short poem. The experience that any artist is attempting to give the audience is the experience of being alive, to be a fellow participant in being. The routine and boredom of the everyday makes the gift of the arts precious.

For example, in Elizabeth Bishop's "The Fish" the poem builds with a list that breaks into a sublime moment, an epiphany for the fisher persona, the idea to let it go free: "the sun-cracked thwarts, / the oarlocks on their strings, / the gunnels—until everything / was rainbow, rainbow, rainbow! / And I let the fish go" (lines 72-76) One finds something similar in Bishop's friend Robert Lowell's "Skunk Hour," even though the persona's epiphany as he approached a "column of kittens" is one that aligns him with the skunk family: "jabs her wedge-head in a cup / of sour cream, drops her ostrich tail, / and will not scare. (lines 46-48). We empathize with the persona and are led to the negative experience in the epiphany.

A more contemporary example of a modern mainstream (white) literary poem might be Billy Collins' "Some Days." In the poem, he calls our attention to the differences in performance between going about as our casual selves and presenting artificial selves at a formal dinner. His use of the empathy to move the reader within his persona's experience to a sublime epiphany is direct by his stating "Very funny, / but how would you like it / striding around like a vivid god, / your shoulders in the clouds, or sitting down there amidst the wallpaper, / staring straight ahead with your little plastic face?" (lines 13-20). This persona is demonstrating a democratic attitude to align himself with the reader's position in the dynamic relationship of poet and reader. In fact, he is suggesting that the reader's position is a superior one to being a celebrated poet. The reader might indeed like sitting with a plastic face being honored.

What makes capitalist poetry the winner is the amount of exposure that people have of it. One remembers "Tony the Tiger says, 'Kellogg's Frosted Flakes. They're Grrreat!'" or the "Have it your way" jingle, but most people haven't even read the lines from "The Fish" or "Skunk Hour," never mind have them memorized. Exposure to these poems or other literary poems (including ones by Whitman and Dickinson) may have been cursory in grade school, but exposure isn't enough. Any music, pop or classical, and the lyrics are flattened made banal in the service of selling and the buying experience and not promoting the experience of living, or of an idea, or of thinking or of an American culture other than scrambling and competing for money.

## FRYE'S FORGOTTEN PROMISE

Long ago, Frye hoped that educated imaginations would protect us from the threat of our falling into an imaginary world that is the world of the social imagination, an "inverted form of imagination" that would distort our sense of reality (141). He suggested that if we educated the imaginations, we would compare ourselves to characters in literature and art and not real people. He pointed out that comparing ourselves to other people was how "ignoramuses" behaved (15). To have built Frye's democratic society would mean citizens as consumers would possess a weak sense of envy and schadenfreude. The society of kinder hearts and educated imaginations has not come to be because it threatens capitalist culture. Because we failed to bring literature and the arts to the greater population, the common language shared by our society is one of advertisements and public relations efforts and not one from a literature and art foundation.

Bishop may honor our origins as animals and lovers of freedom. Lowell's persona may admit his mind is not right and turn the world into black and white. Collins may empathize in a democratic gesture with the reader who isn't being honored at a dinner. However, very few of the democratic masses read, interpret, experience, and study these poems? Whether they are forbidden to or whether they are too busy surviving, reading poetry is low the list of priorities and not encouraged by any democratic institution. The "democratic" masses hum today's equivalent of "We want the world to sing in three-part harmony. It's the real thing," or any other flattened poem pitching envy and desire to own and not to experience or to think.

Without literature and the arts having as much exposure as advertisements nothing in culture matures and nothing becomes truly democratic. Nothing lifts the ape in us to a more emotionally mature and humane being. It turns an empathetic impulse to fantasy and envy. The capitalist poet issues exploitation to separate those who have little money from what they have. The consumer is humiliated through his mimed actions, encouraged to remain a child or worse thoughtless. The society is left to having memorized quite by accident television commercials and sharing nothing existential, nothing cultural, and nothing political aside from capitalist ideology while filling homes with stuff.

Five decades after Frye, Slavoj Žižek in his "The Pervert's Guide to Ideology" with more urgency calls our attention to the social imagination or as he calls it, the "social authority," the "dictator in democracy." He includes public relations and marketing campaigns' "propaganda, publicity, glitz, posters and so on." Žižek is more forceful in his delivery, attempting to let his audience know how our spontaneous relationship to our social world is a seductive "ultimate illusion." He informs us that our illusion is so powerful that "you must be forced to be free," that we don't want to leave ideology's illusion, that there is "extreme violence [in] liberation" from it, and that "freedom hurts" (Pervert's *Guide*). The freedom Žižek speaks of is the same freedom that Frye urges literate people to fight for "to protect us from fall into illusions that society threatens us with." (141)

Given that Frye and later Žižek warned about the illusory power of the social imagination, Jean Baudrillard's "simulacra" theory makes sense. Baudrillard suggests that postmodern global culture exists in a virtual reality or in an effaced reality substituted by constructed images and propaganda when he states, "That it is nevertheless the map that precedes the territory." He calls the illusion "hyperreality" (1). As a result, we are lost in the imaginary world of marketing and public relations campaigns, where capital's reliance on ever greater depletion of raw materials presses for ever greater consumption and exploitation of peoples who lack an educated imagination. In fact, in a recent lecture delivered on March 2nd 2017 at UCLA, Žižek tells us that "capitalism is the point of truth," is "based on instability" has "triumphed," and while it has, it isn't the end of the story ("Courage" 1:47:27). Žižek and Baudrillard explain that now we are embedded in what Frye called the illusion of the social imagination we don't want out, that we are children pathologically living in a world of make believe (Frye 141).

Bernays' capitalist poetry is powerful poetry, memorized, mimed, and hummed. He understood the power of sensibility to influence hearts and minds more than university arts and humanities departments have. He understood without knowing it that "[i]deas don't float in the air, they live in your neuro-circuitry" as George Lakoff puts it (White). Education for self-actualization has been ignored.

What Frye calls educating imaginations is kinds of thinking that allows noticing the nuances of thinking for one's self so as not to get entangled in mob psychology and group-think. This kind of thinking allows one to learn empathy's territory and when compassion is effective, and when a call for compassion is due to nature or preventable man-made issues. By reading and experiencing the wide ranges of literature and art—comedy, romance, tragedy, and irony/satire—one dwells upon what kinds of experiences the world has offered in the past and sometimes forces upon us (Frye 102). Reading these texts fosters empathy but also perspective by way of what has been experienced and thought by others. They assist in problem-solving by giving us how others have dealt with all kinds of problems. Indeed, educating the imagination is the road to self-actualization by making habit of recognizing one's self as different but also a historical being able to impact one's life and the lives of others during one's becoming.

What this kind of thinking also gives us is a perspectival nature, a way of imagining another's subjectivity while distinguishing it from one's own. A lifetime project of building this kind of interiority allows the lifelong student to resist the knee-jerk conclusion for a mind open to processing, for the ability to understand other points of view and even to explore the counter-intuitive and counter arguments. It detects social myths and ideologies of all stripes and distinguishes them from the individual thought process, allowing freedom of thought. Thinking like this is valuable in social situations and in political life. It will be paramount in the future with the new cosmopolitanism, with surveillance capitalism, and with big data and cognitive science where "the-internet-of-everything" and trans-human singularity loom.

## THE ECLIPSE OF BERNAYS AND THE ENLIGHTENMENT

Advertisers in surveillance capitalism are now using addiction code, engagement technologies to race to the bottom of the brainstem to neuro-circuitry by hacking the brain and selling eyeballs. Surveillance capitalism circumvents repressive desublimation and goes for dopamine in all of us as a way to addict us to software for advertisers. Without a strong sense of identity and an ability to think for one's self, educating one's imagination, anyone can now become a member of the herd and many are. "There's a whole playbook of techniques that get used, to get you using the product (smartphones) for as long as possible" (Harris 00:38-00:44). (Kids are often the biggest users.) Tamsin Shaw reports that "behavioral techniques that are being employed by governments and private corporations do not appeal to our reason; they ... change behavior by appealing to our nonrational motivations, our emotional triggers and unconscious biases. If psychologists could possess a systematic understanding of these nonrational motivations they would have the power to influence the smallest aspects of our lives and the largest aspects of our societies" (Shaw 1). As it turns out once the population is addicted to the smartphone and laptop, behavior is shaped.

The Enlightenment has led us into a very threatening era because its founders assumed mature adults were engaged as Postman argued, not treated as children or simply brainwashed. All these decades later, while I have taught in arts and humanities departments, we have failed to rescue our students, citizens who have never gone to college, or ourselves. The arts and humanities for the most part existed within the power structure that gave us cultural shocks, and produced defeatism, learned helplessness, and demoralization and didn't question that structure or think or imagine beyond it. The Enlightenment has led us away from democracy that seemed a byproduct of capitalism to rule blatantly by the wealthy, to oligarchy. The function capitalist poetry played is now being augmented by digital addiction and behavior shaping artificial intelligence.

Perhaps we could see our path to our current situation as one long continued obsessive fascination with science. If we could do that, we could recognize that emphasis, the hyper-attention or over-emphasis on science during the last two centuries. Today, we have pseudo-sciences and scientism seeking legitimacy, merit. If one carefully observes, one might find that techno-capitalists in lab coats infiltrated science laboratories and now pretend to do science in corporate "collaborations," while entrepreneurs pick through the trash outside DARPA to "rent" "inventions" to consumers: the marriage of business and science. The emphasis on analysis and categorization has led us to the valuable basics of life. However, due to science's marriage to business that encourages the military industrial complex where all innovation is good, we lack the deliberative and sentient keel that a more arts and humanities based culture would bring. The innovation is now causing debt that can't be sustained.

We need to acknowledge that science has dominated our attention for at least two centuries. By doing so, we may have an opportunity to recognize our illusion in its promises via capitalism were illusions and allow a totally contingent encounter change our direction, change our culture. The obsession with science is so total that Yuval Noah Harari suggests that the wealthy will begin engineering their genes to move from Homo sapiens to Homo Deus leaving behind for extinction the Homo sapiens who can't afford the engineering, either genetic or computer enhancements of the body. Stephen Hawking was so convinced that this would happen, he has stated, "Once such superhumans appear, there will be significant political problems with unimproved humans, who won't be able to compete." ... "Presumably, they will die out, or become unimportant. Instead, there will be a race of self-designing beings who are improving at an ever-increasing rate" (81).

The instrumentarian thinking associated with science is also behind neoliberalism that has overthrown democracy during the last 40 years prompting Wendy Brown in her book *The Undoing of Demos* to state that "neoliberalism is profoundly destructive to the fiber and future of democracy" and "transmogrifies every human domain and endeavor, along with humans themselves, according to a specific image of the economic. All conduct is economic conduct; all spheres of existence are framed and measured by economic terms and metrics, even when those spheres are not directly monetized." (9, 10) Her book explains Foucault's biopolitics, biology's totalitarian effects on humans, and Giorgio Agamben's three concepts "bios," "zoe," and "homo sacer:" Political life of productivity and making money; bare life, nonpolitical life that isn't productive, makes no money, and is vulnerable as a possible burden on society ("the beastialization of man"); and the life deemed outside society, an outcast, and fair game to anyone to kill, and in "the state of exception" all three can be conflated.

In her book *The Age of Surveillance Capitalism*, Shoshana Zuboff reports that twenty years after our entry into neoliberalism it has given birth to surveillance capitalism. She defines surveillance capitalism as follows:

> Surveillance capitalism is a boundary-less form that ignores older distinctions between market and society, market, and world, or market and person. It is a profit-seeking form in which production is subordinated to extraction as surveillance capitalists unilaterally claim control over human, societal, and political territories extending far beyond the conventional institutional terrain of the private firm or the market. Using Karl Polanyi's lens, we see that surveillance capitalism annexes human experience to the market dynamic so that it is reborn as behavior[.] (514)

Zuboff goes on the explain that technology "is an existential narcotic prescribed to induce resignation" and one that will foster the "seventh extinction," not of nature but of what is "most precious in human nature: The will to will, the sanctity of the individual, the ties in intimacy, the sociality that binds us together in promises, and the trust they breed" (516). She refers to the threat of the "Big Other," what Harari called the "Internet-of-All-Things." He asserts that once this data-processing system "mission is accomplished, Homo sapiens will vanish" (443). If the warnings of Harari, Brown, and Zuboff are not enough to convince writers and thinkers that we are in a kind of lacuna or what Zygmunt Bauman calls an interregnum, then writers and thinkers are naïve. But how do writers of all striped respond to the crisis at hand? I would strongly suggest imagining and then writing different futures for the Homo sapiens, as many as possible to give reader hope and perhaps a model. These voices would be prophetic voices, needed now more than ever. I think of our situation as one outside Plato's Cave and in need of a new ideal, a human story to believe in.

The West has had a tradition of individuals "falling in love" where the subconscious chooses its illusion as a way of needed learning by a couple. In the same vein Western cultures fall in love with ideologies, live and learn the lessons and then become disillusioned but ready to fall in love again. Our disillusionment with capitalism leaves us a lacuna for contingency to sweep us off our feet. However, techno-capitalism's equivalent algorithms for dating websites are threatening our traditional method of nimbly shifting love interests in the West.

## LET'S FALL IN LOVE

The lacuna or interregnum is what Žižek calls "the inconsistent edifice of the logical interconnection of all possible illusion" (4). The West falls in love (as individuals do with each other) but with an ideology that changes our orientation to the world often for generations. The different ideology isn't successive organic growth necessarily but distinctly independent to itself. It has its flaws (and that is what attracts us subconsciously) and sooner or later when the benefits of the ideology have been lived fully and the flaws have been experienced fully also, we release the beloved ideology. At that point we are ready to fall in love again. This is where we are currently in the West: Ready for the contingency of falling in love with a new ideology to take hold. There is a lot to be gained by falling in love: The limits of the illusion and the reality of the particular chosen illusion. Poetry and philosophy may be able to help influence the choice. However, it is also the function of poetry and philosophy to critique the illusory ideology as part of its critical thinking and education of the imagination. No partner in a love affair likes to be told negative things about his/her love.

When someone such as Chomsky points out the flaws of our ideology, he finds it difficult to find a mainstream publisher for his political critique. Mainstream news organizations fully embedded in their ideology find him not worthy of befriending. The critique is vital to the illusion, a reminder, a moment of clarity. He is what Adorno understood as someone not embedded in ideology, someone who thinks for himself and "is considered weak, cowardly, virtually a traitor" by the masses enthralled in the ideology (8). The function of philosophers and poets does serve the function while the loving goes on as a reminder of the illusory nature of loving, a kind of teaching tool and is especially useful as disillusionment sets in.

For instance, William Empson explains the function of literature in *Milton's God*: "The central function of imaginative literature is to make you realize that other people act on moral convictions different from your own…. [A] literary work may present a current moral problem, and to some extent alter the judgement of those who appreciate it by making them see the case as a whole" (261). Frye explains the function of literature as a way "to fight to protect us from falling into the illusions that society threatens us with" (141). Zygmunt Bauman points out the function of literary poets as intermediaries of illusions in his 2016 lecture on cosmopolitanism when he points out the need to understand what we might perceive to be the enemy and remarks, "The way of understanding the enemy is the prerogative of poets, saints, and traitors" (Bauman "Cosmopolitanism"). It seems to be that literary poets are needed more than ever; perhaps there is a respectable place for the arts and humanities in a future global society to remind us of the illusory ideal that are science and technology and to assist in integrating the peoples of the world, to perhaps understand Earth as a spacecraft where Homo sapiens practice space craft.

## WORKS CITED

Adorno, Theodor. *Critical Models: Interventions and Catchwords*. New York: Columbia University Press, 2005.
Agamben, Giorgio. *Homo Sacer: Sovereign and Bare Life*. Stanford: Stanford University Press, 1998.
Alexievich, Svetlana. *Secondhand Time: The Last of the Soviets*. New York: Random House, 2016.
Arendt, Hannah. *Hannah Arendt: For the Love of the World*. 2$^{nd}$ ed., edited by Elisabeth Young-Bruehl, New Haven: Yale University Press, 2004.
Barthes, Roland. *Mythologies*. Translated by Annette Lavers. New York: Hill and Wang, 1972.
Baudrillard, Jean. *Art and Artefact*. 2nd ed., edited by Nicholas Zurbrugg. Newbury Park, California:SAGE Publications, 1998.
Bauman, Zygmunt. "Cosmopolitanism and Challenges of Our Time," YouTube video, 56:43.Posted January 10, 2017.https://www.youtube.com/watch?v=6Bi2h4e3-rI&t=3s.
Bauman, Zygmunt, and Leonidas Donskis. *Liquid Evil*. Cambridge: Polity Press, 2016.
Bernays, Edward. *Propaganda*. New York: Routledge, 1928. Accessed December 1, 2017. http://www.historyisaweapon.com/defcon1/bernprop.html.
Bishop, Elizabeth. "The Fish." in *The Complete Poems: 1927-1979*. New York: Farrar, Straus and Giroux, 1979.
Brodsky, Joseph. "An Immodest Proposal." *On Grief and Reason*. New York: Farrar, Straus & Giroux, 1995.
Brown, Wendy. *Undoing the Demos*. Brookline: Zone Books, 2015.
Chomsky, Noam. "Full Interview: Noam Chomsky on Trump's First 75 Days & Much More." Interview by Amy Goodman, *Democracy Now*!, 5 Apr. 2017, www.youtube.com/watch?v=QT4MO9uQxgc.
——— "What Makes Mainstream Media Mainstream." Z Media Institute, Woods Hole, MA, Jun. 1997. Lecture.
Collins, Billy. "Some Days." in *Picnic, Lightning*. Pittsburgh: University of Pittsburgh Press, 1988.
Danto, Arthur. *After the End of Art*. Princeton: Princeton University Press, 1995.
Empson, William. *Milton's God*. London:Chatto and Windus, 1966.
Felluga, Dino. "Modules on Baudrillard: On Simulation." *Introductory Guide to Critical Theory*. Purdue University. July 17, 2002. Accessed 1 Dec. 2017
https//:www.cla.purdue.edu/english/theory/postmodernism/modules/baudlldsimulTnmainframe. html.
Frye, Northrop. *The Educated Imagination*. Bloomington: Indiana University Press, 1964.
Harari, Yuval, Noah. *Homo Deus*. London: Penguin Vintage, 2015.
Harris, Tristan, "Why Can't We Put Down Our Smartphones?" Interview by Anderson Cooper. *60 Minutes*, CBSN. April 7, 2017, www.cbsnews.com/news/why-cant-we-put-down-our-smartphones-60-minutes/.
Hawking, Stephen. *Brief Answers to the Big Questions*. New York: Bantam Books, 2018.
Heidegger, Martin. "Letter on 'Humanism.'" *Pathmarks*. Edited by W. McNeil. Translated by Frank A. Capuzzi. Cambridge: Cambridge University Press, 1998.
Herman, Edward S., and Noam Chomsky. *Manufacturing Consent*. New York: Pantheon Books, 1988.

Kentucky Fried Chicken. Advertisement. Google image. Accessed 1 Dec. 2017.
www.google.com/search?q=Kentucky+Fried+Chicken+images&newwindow=1&client=gmail&rls=gm&tbm=isch&tbo=u&source=univ&sa=X&ei=AZ2oU7SEHtOysQS5z4HACA&ved=0CB4QsAQ&biw=1366&bih=600.

Marcuse, Herbert. *One-Dimensional Man*. Boston: Beacon Press, 1966.

———. *Eros and Civilization*. Boston: Beacon Press, 1966.

Nike. Advertisement. Google image. Accessed December 1, 2017. www.google.com/search?q=nike+ad+images&client=gmail&rls=aso&authuser=0&source=lnms&tbm=isch&sa=X&ved=0ahUKEwicyO7nh8rUAhVBw4MKHcqGAQsQ_AUICigB&biw=1366&bih=638.

Postman, Neil. *Amusing Ourselves to Death*. New York: Penguin, 1985.

*Pervert's Guide to Ideology*. Directed by Sophie Fiennes, Zeitgeist Films, 2013.

Shaw, Tamsin. "Invisible Manipulators of the Mind." *New York Review of Books*, 20 April 20, 2017.

White, Daphne. "Berkeley Author George Lakoff Says, 'Don't Underestimate Trump'." *Berkeleyside*, May 2, 2017, www.berkeleyside.com/2017/05/02/berkeley-author-george-lakoff-says-dont-underestimate-trump/.

Žižek, Slavoj. "The Courage of Hopelessness." *YouTube*, May 2017,
www.youtube.com/watch?v=aNlW3HnNqlk.

———. *Less than Nothing: Hegel and The Shadow of Dialectical Materialism*. London: Verso, 2012.

Zuboff, Shoshana. *The Age of Surveillance Capitalism*. New York: Public Affairs, 2019.

CHAPTER 9

## Prophetic Voice Now

"See, I think it's quite possible that the 1960s represented the last burst of the human being before he was extinguished."
(Wallace Shawn, 1981)

"But with the end of philosophy, thinking is not also at its end, but in transition to another beginning."
(Martin Heidegger, 1964)

"The truth is the inconsistent edifice of logical interconnection of all possible illusion."
(Slavoj Žižek, 2012)

"We could believe,/ If you told us so"
(Richard Wilbur, 1961)

Early in the 20th century, Paul Valery recognized the loss of a narrative in Europe, in what he called, "the mind of Europe." He wrote, "Every mind of any scope was a crossroads for all shades of opinion; every thinker was an international exposition of thought. There were the works of the mind in which the wealth of contrasts and contradictory tendencies was like the insane displays of light in the capitals of those days: eyes were fatigued, scorched.... (99)" Ernest Becker in his book *Denial of Death* in fact pointed out the importance of myth for all humans when he wrote: "[T]he society everywhere is a living myth of significance of human life, a defiant creation of meaning. (7)"

Yet a few decades ago, Joseph Campbell, a Jungian thinker, told Bill Moyers that the world development was moving too fast for there to be a myth, a vision, or meta-narrative to guide us: "We can't have a mythology for a long, long time to come. Things are changing too fast to become mythologized (31)." His assessment has been supported by postmodernists who have observed that our grand narratives that we have lived by, often without question, have been undercut and that may be a good thing. Postmodern philosophers such as Jean-Francois Lyotard thought that grand narratives muted voices that should be heard especially during globalism's multicultural efforts. Times have changed once again and a grand narrative is needed or we will find ourselves embedded in one not to our liking.

Recently, however, historian Yuval Noah Harari reminds us in *Sapiens* that "(t)he ability to create an imagined reality out of words enabled large numbers of strangers to cooperate effectively. Since large-scale human cooperation is based on myth, the way people cooperate can be altered by changing the myths – by telling different stories." He calls the stories "mythical glue that can be radically altered within two decades. (31 - 38)" In his later book *Homo Deus*, he is less optimistic that such a myth could take hold in these times. Regardless, he and others have been calling for a different one and giving their best efforts to dream up a few candidate narratives that could lead the world culture in a different homo Sapiens-friendly direction. If that isn't a call to fiction writers and poets, I don't know what is. It is time to compose grand narratives or they will be composed for us by unconscious, without deliberation, without debate, behavior.

We have had the Christian story and the Humanist story and are being threatened with the Data story that sees humans as sources of data, data chips for The-Internet-of-All-Things and that is all according to Harari. Harari is a combination Lewis Mumford and Marshall McLuhan. Harari, at times, seems to write with urgency and other times maps the future with a matter of fact that is frightening. It may be to keep his publishers happy (international corporations of course) that he needs to write with a matter of fact tone when writing about capitalism and its future results caused by financial inequity: A new species "homo Deus" that leaves most of us (those without great wealth) behind, eventually extinct.

What has convinced me that the prophetic voice is necessary in the 21 Century is the function that myth plays in our lives as fictions taken as truths. Slavoj Žižek has placed fiction as a concealment supplementing the emptiness of reality (*Less than Nothing* 4). He may declare the core of philosophy is "the path from illusion to critical denunciation" but he goes further to suggest that "philosophy explains why illusions are illusion, [and] also why they are structurally necessary, unavoidable, not just accidents (LTN 10)." Here he agrees with Ernest Becker. The trick is to know the embedded illusion enough to see where it leads, critique it, and then be a kind of advocate for an improved alternative possibility, given the possibilities. The myth needs to be taken for the real by more and more people of influence in a society, not a fairy tale for obfuscation.

He is correct, I believe. In a recent article in *Foreign Policy* James Traub called the United States of America "Decadent and Depraved," and suggests that "in a democracy the distinctive feature of decadence is not debauchery but terminal self-absorption" and goes on to make his analogy between America and Edward Gibbon's description of Rome in 408 A.D (1). So it may be that there is no turning back. Politicians such as Yanis Varoufakis are attempting to influence the hegemonic narrative as it is in the DiEM25 movement. In an earlier essay, I called for an end to the Enlightenment, but not to go back to anything. Instead, I suggested that global culture could embark on a more deliberate way that doesn't drop its load in the lap of ideology-bound techno-capitalist science community who will then declare that our destiny was a matter of our human nature. It is a long shot, but contingent changes in direction have happened in a decade.

In an essay in *New Writing*, I address the need for prophetic voice when I compared Spivak's essay "Reading the World" to The Rolling Stone's "As Tears Go

By" and W. B. Yeats's "Sailing to Byzantium." In my essay "Reading Wisdoms," I use concentric circles to distinguish among folk wisdom, cultural wisdom (both examples of Foucault's empirical order and Spivak's, "we are disc jockeys of an advanced technocracy" to illustrate a breach of the cultural wisdom and the cycle of empirical order, opening a space for visionary thinking and practice. Spivak's insight holds open that space for us to assess what we are doing via capitalism, science, and empire and why. In that space we would need space craft, and that space craft would require the courage of hopelessness and recognizing Utopia as an invention and enactment from the impossible into a new paradigm practice, a different understanding of the condition of the sentient human.

Peter Sloterdijk, a German philosopher calls our period the Anthropocene, where our activity dominates over climate, environment, and nature with the end of the human as a "living" being, becoming. Sociologist Zygmunt Bauman explains our situation in kinder terms, as an interregnum, in particular a divorce between power and politics. Bauman advocates socialism. Slavoj Žižek, a Hegelian philosopher, has been attempting to be a cross between a Lacanian psychologist for cultures (a la Paul Valery) and a Hegelian coach for such different narratives. So, it is acknowledgement of the importance of our linguistic contribution to humans that moves a poet or writer and not spiritual conviction to use the prophetic voice. Prophetic voice in storytelling among humans today, an alternative to the story that threatens us, is vital to the physical survival for all that is left of fauna and flora.

Žižek writes and speaks with urgency. For him the future is happening as a catastrophe now, and we are not prepared for it. Žižek has urged his readers and YouTube listeners to "fall in love all the way" with a different story (Big Think). Many readers don't find him speaking clearly, but he is attempting to not spring from the left without absorbing what needs to be understood from the right. However, it must be kept in mind that any story is wrapped around a response to crises with the tools that are available at the time, so that homo Deus is an attempted solution using the life science tools. Beneath this response of course is the idea that there are other responses to crises and other tools that are available, so that a story or stories might influence the direction and outcome.

My writing here shouldn't be construed as suggesting that those engaged in prophetic vision as having any easy answers. The "framework of literature is one of the loss and regaining of identity" and the visionary writer (a prophetic voice) doesn't tell the reader what happened, but what happens given a situation in which we find ourselves (55, 63 The Educated Imagination). This means that when culture lacks identity, as our global culture lacks today (it never having had one, it now being global), writings with vision attempt to construct an identity for it. The prophetic voice attempts to advocate for a narrative that one would like to live within, knowing that it won't be perfect should the narrative be adopted. It is a fiction of course. There isn't anything magic or mystical about it. It is about knowing history, current events, and how life on the planet has seemed to have gone on in a general way and then applying those perceptions to the situation as the writer understands it. The writer could be misunderstanding the cultural situation or seeing it as in the eyes of other intelligent people. What has to be factored out is the biases and illusion of the writer. If he or she is seeing the dialectic of the time clearly and understands how its dynamism works, the vision may be accurate and helpful. However, there is always contingency that can change the narrative completely.

Any different narrative will probably address three disciplines at the heart of our current situation I would suggest: Economics, science, and art. The first illusion is capitalism. Capitalism is a life and death game with devastating waste of resources and humans in particular. The illusion is one of "deserves." By emphasizing deserves we attempt to use ethics and superficial Darwinism to rationalize the guilt in luck. For instance, one person works hard his whole life and achieves little while another never works a day in his life due to being born a trust fund inheritor and receives all the benefits of wealth. Luck or chance has much more to do with our situation on Earth than "deserves," though being a literal trust fund recipient is in large measure (if not totally) a matter of chance. We continue to follow Edward Bernays' capitalist propaganda narrative that gives the illusion of freedom while the CEOs and political elite dictate our tastes and desires, our dreams and wishes. All important choices are made for us, while we pretend we made them.

Capitalism may act as a buffer against slavery; its rules for deserves include 500% earning deferential and earnings while one sleeps. One strategy "the deserves" use against those who don't deserve is John Milton's "They who have put out the people's eyes reproach them of their blindness." Blaming the victim allows the wealthy to sleep. Consider fast food and its benefits to health. While it solves a hunger problem today, it causes a health problem tomorrow. The illusion that the poor can also eat out gives them a false sense of wealth. Once deserves learn that behavior, it is easy to "learn to predict a fire with unerring precision / Then burn the house down to fulfill the prediction" as Milosz once wrote of Stalin's rule (85). These are merely a couple of strategies at hand. The themes of deserves and luck play out in neuroscience and other areas of life as well.

Addressing science in the narrative would mean addressing the change from language being communication via conversation to one of language as information. What is being missed in these suggestions is that science has only been allowed to explore and develop in areas that capitalism will pay for, in areas that promise money making. Zygmunt Bauman put it this way, "problems are solved for the wealthy not for humanity (Personally Speaking)." If money sources were to permit exploration down other avenues without worry of profit, we might have found at this point that our situation isn't so dire. We may have found an exit ramp a century ago. Without capitalism and empire, science might serve the greater good. A new narrative that promotes genuine aesthetic experience might include a strategy for education and bringing forth art and eliminating the dream of cyborgs.

The arts are the one sure way to the peak experience for humans. The experience of being alive is the peak experience that combines imagination and intellect. It provides each audience member of possible human experiences. It also reminds that no amount of living can compare to a sense of purpose from a developed talent for sharing. One could argue that to travel through life and not experience the momentary feeling of being alive is to have not lived life fully. Through art these human peak experiences are found in one of three sublime experiences that if s/he could s/he would choose to live often. They include the masculine sublime where the physical world overwhelms the senses; the feminine sublime that more domestically exposes the limits of the senses; and the postmodern sublime that brings forth one or both by way of the continuing presence of "now" or what Žižek calls the real. The artist achieves the peak experience of the sublime and shares it, reminding the audience that each can achieve a similar experience in the work of their lives, work that they make their purpose. It would be difficult to skirt these three issues (economic, scientific, and artistic) in any distinct narrative.

One might also think of the prophetic voice as completing the function of what Northrop Frye called educating the imagination. Frye feared that the power of the illusionary force that he called the "social imagination" found in propaganda and advertising led to mob psychology by the masses. He saw how the mob (now called consumers or pop culture in general) could easily fall under the social imagination's power and into delusion. He wrote, "The first thing our imaginations have to do for us, as soon as we can handle words well enough to read and write and talk, is to fight to protect us from falling into the illusions that society threatens us with." (89, Educated Imagination).

We might think of his recommending a defensive posture and also a strategy of shaping a more humane culture that he articulates in his books and the books of all literary culture. Today, prophetic voices would be the vanguard for bringing about a more sentient society, humane culture. The method would be one of our constructing and posited mainly by the arts, a living culture churning in self-correction dialectic where illusion is critiqued and an improved illusion is generated. What makes it different from our current dialectic is that the arts would take a more prominent role, influencing decisions and direction.

We poets and writers are in an emergency situation, and so much depends on us putting forth visions via language. It is our combined contributions that make a language after all. A call for prophetic voice does mean that the writer's other job at the other end of thinking needs greater emphasis going forward. In fact, it might be understood as a matter of emphasis or accent, where the poet responded to a shift in culture. One can find the elements of prophetic voice in Auden's "Unknown Citizen," Lowell's "Waking Early Sunday Morning," Gluck's "Mock Orange" or "The Triumph of Achilles," Harjo's "A Map to the Next World," Walcott's "Star Apple Kingdom," Ashbery's short "Thoughts of a Young Girl" and so many other lyric, confessional, and persona poems however one defines their styles. Sylvia Plath's poem "Daddy" is a prophetic anthem of sorts for women in the future prepared to say "Daddy, daddy, you bastard, I'm through." These poems are critiques and peeks at alternatives. One can't speak to the prophetic voice during the era in which I was brought up without speaking to Allen Ginsburg.

His poem "Howl" in particular is meant to be prophetic and it is in tone and is a harkening of gay liberation, but it misses the mark with its drawing on the spiritual realm and blaming women. Instead of blaming a fellow victim of the power-knowledge discourse of the day, Ginsberg might have made headway into making his poem a truly visionary work by hitting the mark with his blame: Heterosexual ideology, men pledging heterosexuality to settle a matter of sexuality and gender, not women whose minds one could argue were being destroyed in vastly greater numbers than those men in Ginsberg's poem. Even advocating the liberation of women would have assisted the argument that the poem was making. One might argue that he was a product of the fifties and modernism so he wasn't privy to our thinking. However, that is precisely what makes one question whether this poem is a visionary postmodern poem and question whether it deploys bad ideology if one is interested in liberation. In any case, Ginsberg's moving beyond blaming the "heterosexual dollar" to blame women may be troublesome for anyone reading the poem from 1970 on and especially insightful women and men (14).

The "minds" he speaks of in "Howl" cue me to what are referred to these days as the redundant workers, irrelevant, not considered, useless. That doesn't mean that they were or are. What it does mean is that capitalism has a limited number of places for educating students and for useful people who are usually anointed (with few exceptions) by Ivy League status in the meritocracy. Other minds, regardless of how intelligent, able, accurate in thought, promising in future are disregarded. We can see those disregarded clearly in what is called neo-liberalism today. The message sent to those not "needed" is one of worthlessness. In Ginsberg's day as in ours it drives people to depression, insanity, and suicide. It is best not to believe any cultural narrative that divides and defines people. The disenfranchisement of people is capitalism exposing its weakness, one of its limitations in its prophetic narrative, neo-liberalism's "there are no alternatives."

The task of affecting change by way of the prophetic voice in literature may be futile or it may have some small influence on something like Dataism. However, it is up to writers and thinkers to attempt a different direction for humans and the humanities if we as humans wish for a place in the future. We can't just sit back and hope for a contingent event to move us away from disaster. Our distinct direction may embrace lyric poetry's ability to shepherd becoming. The metaphors used by the above-mentioned philosophers explain how they may assist poets and writers in delineating an exit ramp, a fork in the road. Notice how they resort to poetry (metaphor) to express their ideas. The way for the practicing prophetic humanist who writes is one of crafting myths that move from the hopelessness of our current nuclear, ecological, bio-genetic, economic, and political threats to one of global planetary humanism that embraces all as fellow animals and vegetation traveling through the cosmos while calling Earth home for being and becoming.

We, of course, have the mainstream media orchestrated against such storytelling. While these voices would be ideal for spreading prophetic voices, these electronic and print media outlets are international corporations that have nothing to gain by adopting a different story to supplant the story that they are attempting to convince us is the only story. Our best thinkers find it almost impossible to be published by a mainstream publisher: Noam Chomsky, Chris Hedges, and Slavoj Žižek. They, as does global finance, dictate our dreams, dictate our reality. The mainstream media intimidation, coercion, and ignor-ance are an attempt to convince us that composing a different story that addresses the larger more vital concerns than their profit is futile. The prospects are dismal, but we are desperate. However, the more writers who tell prophetic stories the greater the chance a different story will take hold in the public imagination as a distinctly new way. Some narratives will conflict with one another and others will overlap or amend a narrative that may overwhelm the mainstream resistance.

Recently, Sloterdijk has been advocating that our story needs to change to one of understanding the planet as Earth, the spaceship that uses its space station as a tool for self-reflection, as our conscience and defines it: "To have a conscience means to know that one is observed from a deep off-center position and pervaded by it." He goes further suggesting that "the authority of off-center observation [needs to be] deep enough to be able to for a counterbalance to the egocentricity of local interests."("Deep Observation" 109 & 110) Sloterdijk is a conservative philosopher. However, his idea for the next story has my attention and at this time in a general way has my support. What I like first about the prophetic myth is how one can play with the metaphor. A space station needs a spaceship and spaceship can be also thought of as "space craft," that what we need on planet Earth is space craft, a kind of fengshui for all living things, including humans being, cooperating in asceticisms, a shared practice in survival.

Žižek speaks to the same issue when he writes about the commons, what we share as social beings: The ecology, our biology, public spaces, and intellectual property. These commons are shared resources, not for private exploitation. By using something like fengshui, the planet becomes more of a public park or garden than mining opportunity and dumping ground when all species except the rich suffer the consequences of the rich's addiction to money.

Once the space craft story begins to take hold, the spacecraft part of the new myth might take off sort-to-speak. Or perhaps we would need to lead with "spacecraft" to get the point across that we live on Planet Limited and that humans are prepared to acknowledge it and wish to not possess among its members endangered species including the human being variety. Approaching the problem this way, allows the human to recognize the sincerity of bio-genetics as well. Harari and Žižek have been attempting to call our attention to what has been taking place in the biological sciences. They and other speculators warn that the wealthy will be the ones able to genetically alter their babies so that a whole new superior species will be lording over whoever remains as human slaves. We may have thought the threat to the future of humanity might be robotics and algorithms. Perhaps, but genetic engineering promises to leave behind for extinction anyone who is not a billionaire. Perhaps, one can see the urgency for a different story, a different myth. My prophetic voice may be useful here as those were when calling for what became known as the Enlightenment centuries ago.

It is this urgency that should warn us that we have wandered off the path of human being and are living in dangerous times for all the reasons mentioned earlier having forgotten the "being" in human being, being as a verb of presence, of becoming, not sheltered or hidden by human nature. Sloterdijk's book *You Have to Change Your Life* warns and also suggests a pathway through practice, as does Žižek's more abstract *Less than Nothing*. For this reason, I have taken a second look at two of Heidegger's basic metaphors: "Man is not the lord of beings; man is the shepherd of being" and his "language is the house of being" (239). By unpacking these metaphors I hope to make greater sense of them. However, from here on I am outlining my thinking more abstractly as I continue to bring detail of the vision to give voice to.

For Heidegger, language is important, and a human has a very different meaning from a human being. "Being" is a verb as in becoming and not a noun with "human" as an adjective. Being is always the first verb that others verbs may be attached to, such as "a human being and working at the conveyor belt." Placing being first presents the individual over its nature, the human. This is what he meant by being as presence in the world, where being recognizes each presence in a world that threatens us with planetary homelessness, where technology sweeps us along after it.

I have tried to articulate why it is vital that the prophetic voice by writers be heard. Many questions will go unanswered. Perhaps our trauma that sent us on the path of will to power stems from a belief that we had to conquer nature, so that we might be comfortable on the planet (or in our cave). Whatever the cause of our addiction to power (and its symbol, money), we are up against the wall now, especially 80 percent of us. As waves of environmental refugees and asylum seekers amass on shores and boarders, it is clear that they are luckier than those left behind. Only those living in great comfort (the 20 percent bubble) wouldn't recognize the suffering of those asylum seekers and the ones left behind them.

The goal, the lowest bar is to have being deliberate to develop the sentient aspects of our human nature and share the natures of fauna and flora we would share the planet, to relieve or minimize suffering, and to have a narrative composed that enables and that supports this goal. The prophetic voice in writing can be a force. Žižek interestingly thinks that the Holy Spirit in Christianity should be viewed secularly as the result of the death of Christ, God; that then puts the responsibility onto the people alone for bringing forth a compassionate and sentient world, making everyone a member the Holy Spirit. He sees his amendment as a way of leaving the religious story and moving on to a story where people recognize their ability to control their lives and take responsibility for stewardship of the Earth.

## WORKS CITED

Agamben, Giorgio. *Homo Sacer.* Stanford: Stanford University Press, 1995.

Bauman, Zygmunt. "Personally Speaking:" Conversations with Zygmunt Bauman. Film 3.interview with Martin Smith. Dibb Directions, Feb 16, 2017.

Becker, Ernest. *Denial of Death.* New York: The Free Press, Macmillan Publishers,1973.

Campbell, Joseph, with Bill Moyers, edited by Betty Flowers. *The Power of Myth.* New York: Doubleday, 1988.

Frye, Northrop. *The Educated Imagination.* Bloomington: Indiana University Press, 1964.

Ginsberg, Allen. *Howl and other Poems.* San Francisco: City Lights Pocket Poets, No. 4. 1956.

Harari, Yuval Noah. *Homo Deus: A Brief History of Tomorrow.* London: Vintage Penguin Random House, 2016.

———. *Sapiens.* London: Vintage Penguin Random House, 2011.

Heidegger, Martin. "Letter on 'Humanism." *Pathmarks.* Edited by W. McNeil. Translated by Frank A. Capuzzi. Cambridge: Cambridge University Press, 1998.

Klooster, Jacqueline. *Poetry as a Window and Mirror: Positioning the Poet in Hellenistic Poetry.* Boston: Brill, 2011.

Milosz, Czeslaw. "Child of Europe." *New and Collected Poems.* New York: Harper Collins Publishers, 1988.

Milton, John. *An Apology for Smectymnuus with the Reason of Church-Government.* www.oll.libertyfund.org/titles/milton-the-prose-works-of-john-milton-vol-1

Murphy, Rich."Reading Wisdoms." *New Writing: The International Journal for the Practice and Theory of Creative Writing.* Volume 9: Number 3. 2012.

Shawn, Wallace and Gregory, Andre. "My Dinner with Andre." Dir. Louis Malle. Saga Productions Inc. Oct. 1981. 1:21:48-1:21:56 &1:20:51 - 1:21:22

Sloterdijk, Peter. *You Must Change Your Life: On Anthropotechnics*, translated by Wieland Hoban. Malden: Cambridge: Polity Press, 2013.

———. "Rules for the Human Zoo," *Environment and Planning D: Society and Space* 2009, volume 27, pages 12-28.

———. "Deep Observation," (106-110) *What Happened in the 20$^{th}$ Century?* Cambridge: Polity Press, 2018.

Spender, Stephen. *Poetic Vision and Modern Literature.* Lecture. Audio-Forum, Sound Seminars, 1953.

Traub, James. "The United States of America is Decadent and Depraved." *Foreign Policy.* Dec. 19, 2017. http://foreignpolicy.com/2017/12/19/the-united-states-of-america-is-decadent-and-depraved/

Valery, Paul. *Paul Valery: An Anthology.* Bollingen Series XLV.A, Ed. James R. Lawler. Princeton: Princeton University Press, 1977.

Žižek, Slavoj. "The Courage of Hopelessness." YouTube video, 1:47:27. Posted May 23, 2017. https://www.youtube.com/watch?v=aNlW3HnNqlk.

———. *Less Than Nothing: Hegel and the Shadow of Dialectical Materialism.* London: Verso, 2013.

———. "Big Think." www.youtube.com/watch?v=OabTK7y7d6E

CHAPTER 10

# The Acts of a Solitary Thinker and the Fragile Absolute: A Case Study

> "The most that any one of us can seem to do is to fashion something—an object or ourselves—and drop it into the confusion, make an offering of it, so to speak, to the life force."
> (Ernest Becker, 1973)

Beginning with Kierkegaard, psychologists and philosophers tell us that anxiety is the root, the impetus of all emotions and that all other anxieties lead back to the anxiety of death and the despair of our purposelessness. Anxiety and despair either drives us or crushes us, and if it crushes us it does so that we don't even know that we are in despair. The psychological defenses for the anxiety so protective that many people can travel through life without consciously confronting it. The more one thinks of his/her human condition in anxiety, the greater influence both anxiety and despair has in one's life. Solitude is not only a part of the human condition it is required to experience the anxiety and despair. That is why so many people seek out others, medication, and neurotic ways to keep busy. They fear the anxiety.

The anxiety, of course, is our insignificant and purposeless lives on an insignificant planet in an unknown cosmos. The receiver of the anxiety early in life, and who doesn't have strong psychological defenses at that moment, will attempt to compensate for it as a habit and practice disciplined. This response can often lead to habitually sublimating the anxiety through compensation. It is a first wound that is severe enough to bring about existential anxiety and despair. The wound that is also called the "Hegelian wound" can have an impact on one that it becomes the drive that motivates one the rest of one's life through successes and failures. The wound or "Hegelian wound" (the wound of nature to the spirit that begins the dialectic between them) can have an impact on one that it becomes the drive that motivates one the rest of one's life through successes and failures. In fact, the wounded knows failure very well because s/he has learned through the wound that in the end failure is all. The anxiety is a warning of what is to come but is now sublimated into motivation of practice related to compensation. The drive that has one's death as its motivator is sometimes called the excess of the death drive that carries the spirit or memory of the person after his/her death.

The wound's lifetime impact probably won't be visible until later. However, with certain encouragements and opportunities, push and pull of life's experiences the wounded, who is compensating (and may not need to anymore), is what Heidegger would call becoming until the life experiences Nietzsche's acrobat and has become as

Socrates would say superior to himself. The journey of becoming in this way is a solitary one and is what Slavoj Žižek means by "the fragile absolute." The fragile absolute could end up providing a great contribution to human beings or simply be a person looking back and recognizing how superior s/he is from what promised to be the arc of his/her life at the start. When looking back upon one's life and sees the once miserable self and its likely fate, the contrast in becoming that is the fragile absolute is clear and enough to fill a person's heart. The overall experience is Maslow's self-actualization that brings about peak experiences or flow and also self-realization, when one recognizes what one has made of him/herself.

What I am calling the fragile absolute and attributing to Žižek is the individual who responds to a psychic wound in a way that moves him/her beyond the Freudian pleasure principle to the death drive and so compensates and over compensates for the wound, driven so that his/her very daily activity and interests put them outside the social order. These outcasts are not organized nor do they seek organization but recognize within the works they are doing to be united in struggle against or in spite of the social order. Outside the order, the fragile absolute behavior is unpredictable given the norms of the order within society. Žižek goes further with this idea. However, for my purposes the above will do.

So as I see it, there are ingredients or stages that we experience when becoming, in order to become superior to ourselves, acrobats as Nietzsche says, living and fulfilling the Žižek fragile absolute. They are as follows:

- Solitude (necessary for wound and individual growth);
- Hegelian wound (initial and occasional existential anxiety);
- drive (motivation to compensate or fill the gap, heal the wound);
- (mastery via) practice and discipline through success and failure;
- self-actualization (the flow and peak experiences);
- self realization (self assessment);
- the end or death of the fragile absolute, the human being superior to him/herself; and
- the death drive excess (the motivator of projects complete, projects incomplete, and symbolize one's achievement).

I am writing this autobiographical account of my development as a member of the fragile absolute. What wounded me was not being born without arms or being molested. My wound is merely an example from which I might speak with authority. I wish to support what I believe Žižek means by the fragile absolute in his book *Less than Nothing* and its importance in the contemporary global interregnum. I am writing this account while reading Peter Sloterdijk's *You Must Change Your Life*. So the lens of my understanding of both thinkers is influencing my purpose. Variations on a theme that ended the 1960 movements went something like this: "Change your own life first" or "If everyone changes his own life, he changes the world." My reading of these two thinkers is that they are attempting to explain the how and the why readers need to commit to the changing their lives in these desperate times. Both men are old enough to remember the 60s.

My case study of my life is not a scientific study but recognition that these stages to self-actualization / self-realization have been the core ingredients to my life. Again, I am using my minor example to outline what Žižek means in an individual life. There is a certain amount of needed narcissism in our solitude of becoming, but most of the time that impulse can be restrained from vocalization beyond the flesh in solitude so that we call it self-care or *amour de soi*. I will attempt to give full explanations and descriptions of my experiences as I moved through each stage.

## SOLITUDE AND HEGELIAN WOUND

I tossed and turned sweaty late one night having not been able to get to sleep because I was wondering about the night sky, my birth, my being, my death and the purpose of being alive. I must have been seven the first evening this kind of questioning happened to me. If my dad had been an astronomer or a biologist, I may have become a scientist given the answer he may have given me, but I have no regrets there. I went downstairs, woke my parents, and told them of my thoughts. My dad was a working-class guy who was taught to be callous around emotion. He simply dismissed me with, "go back to bed and go to sleep." I went back to bed, but of course, could not go back to sleep until the sun came up and then it was breakfast time. It turned out to be a positive experience.

This episode was the first of many sleepless nights. Their overwhelming nature taught that I was alone with them, and later that I had little to lose by "shooting for the stars." My wondering became bedrock and my dad's response confirmed for me that I was alone with the anxiety of my awe regarding my existential situation. It also confirmed that this is where my identity, separate from his, lay: individuation. Under the cosmic eye, other judgmental eyes are less important. The experience was my wound. When the thoughts occurred during the day, I distracted myself with my wit, making jokes and language games that also compensated for my lack of answers to my questions. The experience was vital to setting me on my path to poetry.

I actually began my practice of writing on my own early enough that in fifth grade I wrote and drew the contents of several issues of a magazine, each hand written and drawn. I would make two or three of the same "issue" and pass them around the class. The positive feedback (whether sincere or out of politeness) I received pushed me further into the practice of using my imagination and expressing its results in writing: Stories, jokes, imagined battle scenes from World War II. Though this was a small practice, common perhaps, it set me on a course that would a few years later solidify my decision to write my whole life. I can remember thinking at a very young age that all I needed was a pencil (even a stubby one) and a little paper, and I could write anywhere. My second experience was perhaps an experiment in acting out the roles of writer and publisher because I distributed the publication to students around the room.

When I was 13, my mother's brother was hit by a trailer truck and killed. Joe dabbled in the arts and wrote while also later struggling with brain cancer. He was very kind to me while I was young and got me interested in outdoor sports. For me at the time he was my subconscious mentor. For birthdays and Christmas, I had received fishing poles, skis, footballs, etc. In fact, his mentorship had such an impact on me that my adolescent mind noted that he was 33 when he died, the same age a Christ. That is how powerful his influence was for me at 13. After his death, along with his other arts equipment (easel, brushes, paints, typewriter, and trumpet), I received a memoir manuscript written about his father who remains the hero of the family mythology and perhaps rightly so. My receiving the typed pages in a deep manuscript box was as though I were receiving a relay baton in a relay race of life and death significance. His death propelled me further down poetry's road. The death of my uncle, my hardworking grandfather soon after, and then the deaths of the Kennedys and Martin Luther King shook my adolescent world. These deaths woke me to my own time limitations on this planet if the sweaty nights hadn't already done that.

During my middle school years, at the same time my uncle died, I experienced the lesson of Job for the first time. The lesson of Job is of course a recognition that justice doesn't exist and there is no order, no big other who wishes to or can make things right. These are the years when smaller male students spend their lunch money on "insurance" to ensure that they would be less likely to be harassed, humiliated, or beaten. I witnessed horrendous behavior. I lacked resources to understand or cope with the experience perhaps due to a more privileged and unworldly upbringing by parental willed-ignorance. However, when students arrive to seventh grade on motorcycles, control the classroom, and beat a teacher, one learns this isn't a serious school, not even to socialize a generation. To me, my landing in the classroom of this school seemed to have been a practical joke. I was made clear that it wasn't a practical joke when even the bus ride to school was a place for intimidation and acting out with violence family desperations. What I was learning was that I was responsible for whatever I was going to learn.

As a skinny suburban boy with two sisters to "protect," I met the progeny of WWII's battle fatigued post-traumatic stressed veterans. Many veterans were psychologically wounded and then wounded family members. Soldiers and veterans were considered cowards to admit to the post-traumatic distress or battle fatigue. They were even encouraged to take their own lives if they couldn't handle the stress when leaving the service. I imagine many did take their own lives.

However, many vets tortured their own families and police would escape involvement by saying, "It is a family matter." Those angry children would come to school along with those who simply hadn't eaten or having been abused and shamed for a host of other reasons. Learning would not go on here and anything that purports to have been teaching was a charade. At best it was crowd control and at worse intimidation. Freud hadn't arrived in the USA middle or working classes. Needless to say, I learned what I needed to learn: education was not something that is given to one. That exercise, that practice was one done on one's own. If anyone there had an education, it wasn't being used or given away. The students who may have made it through the system and on to college were few whose parents had sent them on that mission. However, I was certainly traumatized by the experience.

While in middle school, I took trumpet lessons. My dad, and uncles, all of them, played the trumpet. One uncle played at clubs and weddings. The lifestyle got to him or he sought the lifestyle and drank and smoked himself to death. What was important for me was first, my entering the "men's club" of music in my family and the ten years of practicing, even if it weren't as serious as it should have been on my part, gave me an appreciation of sound, music, and rhythm. My early idea was to write words and lyrics for music groups. However, my friends who played music in high school went off to Vietnam.

My interest in writing music faded quickly when entering college for music. I recognized how I had wasted whatever talent I had by not taking the trumpet lessons seriously earlier on. My fellow musicians at college were far superior to me which discouraged me even further from moving in this direction. Then I remembered my thinking that all I needed was a stubby pencil to do the work that satisfies me most. Music gave me a sense of rhythm when writing, but my solace, again, were words. My failure to learn trumpet and with education in general were not as vital as time went on.

## DRIVE AND PRACTICE

During my adolescence, I naturally felt as though I was behind in learning and needed to catch up. It was a general anxiety around education. In my late teens I began a practice of always reading a book of poetry, a book of fiction, and a book of nonfiction. I always carried one with me in case I had time to myself. Later, in the late 60s and 70s, records and cassettes in my book bag were not of music but of lectures, poetry, and novels I would borrow from the libraries from Boston, North and listen to when driving. With little faith in education and little encouragement from home, I wrote off serious engagement in college and charged ahead. Taking courses in literature and poetry and poetry writing only, I soon found myself again on my own. I read what was on syllabi, what was in bibliographies and indexes of the books I read. Along with my reading, I of course began writing daily. My attitude to anyone who befriended me was "I am moving in this direction; you are welcome to travel with me and leave at any time." With that kind of attitude, I was alone not necessarily because I wanted to be. It was a lousy attitude, but I was able to read and write, to practice until I had praxis, a habit, a way of life.

Lewis Mumford, Robert Frost in particular, though there were others, fed me hope. They were successful writers without having a college degree. There were other heroes also: Samuel Beckett, Robert Lowell, W. B. Yeats, Arnold Toynbee, Ernest Becker, William Blake, John Ashbery, Saul Bellow, and William Faulkner were a few. However, Frost was so early an influence that I always thought that I would teach someday as he did. I had no idea of how that was going to happen. However, I must have had a shortcut in mind, publishing my way there. I was certainly in need of a steady job. In fact, I had known of other writers becoming faculty members without any degree. Faulkner, who studied Greek tragedy while working as a Postmaster, was one I believe. My idea was to obtain a graduate degree without an undergraduate degree and see whether my publication background and the degree brought me to a teaching position.

A few years of writing had me submitting poems to journals around the country, and while I received many rejection letters, I was soon being published in a few literary journals each year, just enough to feed my dopamine needs. For ten years, twelve years I read and wrote and went through a marriage. I think I had selfish down well, single-minded to not be behind, to succeed whatever that meant. By the time I was 30, I was publishing regularly but lacked a published book or any official credentials from the meritocracy in which I lived.

## Practice and Discipline through Success and Failure 1

The first door opened to me when with a dossier and my publishing record I applied to four graduate programs for creative writing and was accepted by all of them. By this time in my life I had four children and a second wife. Three of the four programs were out of state and two were not universities. My thinking at the time was that for my purposes a university degree would be stronger than a degree from a college. The out of state university's program was an MFA, but to move there with my family seemed impossible. The instate university's program was an MA program that sold itself as one of the oldest and the equivalent of an MFA. It boasted in national publications a list of student who went off to university teaching, and along with Nobel winners, it boasted of its program when Robert Lowell taught Sylvia Plath, Anne Sexton, etc. Robert Lowell was an important draw for me. At the time George Starbuck (director) and Derek Walcott were the poetry workshop facilitators. The decision was easy; I attended Boston University. (BU's program is now an MFA program.)

My time at Boston University was one of great trials while having good friendships with both poets. My writing was very different from the other students, but what challenged me was working to support a family and taking graduate-level literature classes. What gave me confidence was the encouragement I received from George and Derek. By the second semester they were promoting my poetry to publishers, writing letters of introduction, and writing wonderful notes on my manuscripts. One that George wrote I keep close to me even today. It finishes with "I only want to suggest to you that your unchronicled, implicit ambition may be THAT BIG: an unprecedented thing." One could interpret the statement in many ways, and I have over the decades but it speaks of my subconscious drive at the time. I am not certain whether he would say that my achievement was very big, but have used the note as a spark to keep me going when low. Derek would write in a letter of support for publication: "He has earned his individuality by concentration, by a sense of sacrifice." Derek wrote this after telling me that it would take me 30 years to get a book published. He was correct. Both these men were members of the fragile absolute who recognized another who was making his way. They too were men without much in the line of credentials, except of course for their work.

The second door that was opened to me was obtaining my first full-time teaching position at Bradford College, a college opened for 200 year in Haverhill, MA. Before being hired I was a technical editor for the Commonwealth of Massachusetts. Twice each year for two or three years I would send out letters and a resume to every college and university English Department in New England: Once in January and once in August. My thinking was that I may be offered an adjunct position, especially in August when movement of faculty took place, or maybe in January a chair would put my material in with full-time prospects. Yes, I was naïve.

After two years of receiving these letters some chairs asked me to come and be a workshop facilitator for a day or to read and answer questions about my work in a class. But I then got a call in August first to teach an advanced essay class in the following spring at Bradford College and then a week before classes were to begin I was asked if I were interested in a full-time position. I jumped at the opportunity, and though I took a sizable cut in pay, I was pleased to have the opportunity. I rose to associate professor teach writing and literature courses, and then after 14 years I was there when the college closed its doors forever in 2000.

## PRACTICE AND DISCIPLINE THROUGH SUCCESS AND FAILURE 2

The closing was my first experience of professional loss, loss or a professional home, loss of colleagues. During the loss, a colleague who had also experienced divorce as I had, pulled me aside the day that college announced its imminent closure. From our second floor offices we watched faculty and staff scattering to their cars after the announcement after which they were to try to enjoy a Thanksgiving holiday. He said, "There will be many divorces for folks and many will have to find work all around the country, but for you and me, it's just another blip on the radar screen." Whenever after this experience I watched the last scene with the police chief and Bogart walking into the fog in the movie Casablanca, I thought of his words. In fact, it was through his committee I was first hired there. Through his tutelage, I learned quite a lot about higher education, writing programs, and by his actions when to provide opportunity for an acrobat becoming, for someone living the fragile absolute. We have stayed in touch after he moved to another state and found success there.

Looking back I see events that should have angered me or crushed my spirit, and at the time, I shook them off while continuing to work, indeed seeing them as "blips on the radar screen." However, I have come to have felt the impact of regret and frustration as everyone does later in life. Perhaps now I feel the emptiness that the loss of those colleagues left for me. My regrets are over job losses, especially the ways that I had experienced the losses of colleagues and workmates. The first teaching position I lost because a college that educated students for two-hundred years closed.

Another loss was one where a college promotion committee "unanimously," and with "strong recommendation," "enthusiastically" nominated me and put forth my promotion to full professor only to have the president of the college deny it and then lay me off (fired?) with a year's salary. What I lost in both cases were communities of academics and fellow writers and thinkers. However, I was able to see these roadblocks or detours as a part of plowing forward and as none of my business in the long run. My business then was and still is fulfilling whatever promise I had as a writer and thinker regardless of the smaller spirits attempting to slow or stop me. The stubborn drive may be vital to writers, creative people or all people.

## Solitude, Thinking, and Practice

The solitude I have been currently experiencing is different from isolation I have experienced in the past. However, this is not a complaint; other than my life companion, company is not needed just as it isn't needed to sooth existential loneliness; one accepts it because all human beings live it. One simply deals with the dread or tries to sublimate it. In the past, my isolation was a necessary one of the writer alone getting the writing done among (somewhere out there) other writers and thinkers doing something similar. I may have been contributing something unique and hoped that I was, but I had little way of knowing. So I kept plowing ahead and found solace in others with whom I engaged professionally or with whom I socialized on occasion. The aloneness now is different and may be because I have plowed out into ground I have not plowed before, or I have ventured into an area that isn't familiar at all to me but an area of my choosing. I am a kind of pioneer to it, and it is precisely this work that makes me superior to my earlier self.

It is legend that Immanuel Kant, a bachelor and fellow German, was famous for his daily walks precisely at 3:30pm in Königsberg, so that he could think. The feeling of being alone, isolated, seems to be one experienced and needed by thinkers, writers, and artists especially when they are articulating something unique or different. I am not suggesting that I have something vitally important to add to the conversation of writers and thinkers. I may, and that would be fine with me. However, Peter Sloterdijk warns that "By wanting to settle exclusively in the sphere in which he performs his tricks, he ends his relationship with the rest of the world and withdraws to his precarious heights. (YMCYL 68)" I now understand the Promethean anguish that a fewer number of writers feel unless they are in uncharted, far reaches of their thinking in their work. It doesn't mean one's offering is more profound than another's. That may happen, but more importantly it means that the person may be thinking unique thoughts or thinking in unique ways for him/herself.

Hannah Arendt called this kind of thinking, "thinking without banisters." Thinking without banisters is thinking where if anyone was there before, he/she left no way to get there or return, where there is nothing to hold on to, nothing to refer to. Perhaps it is what Wittgenstein meant with his ladder analogy. It must have been what Heidegger meant by "the task of thinking" in his "Letter on 'Humanism.'" My naming philosophers and their ideas are banisters. Thinking without them can't be done in a crowd and engaging in conversations or with a face fixed to a Smartphone screen. One needs to be alone to think thoughts that others may not have ventured into. Heidegger of course was doing precisely that in his essay and suggesting that thinking was important now that for him metaphysics was no more.

In fact, in a recent lecture novelist Will Self argues that isolation is necessary for serious composition. Needless to say that no one can guess what the thinker's thoughts are when that thinking is genuine, unique and actively engaging. The person is on the margins of the symbolic order, especially if that person is a poet. Ideas take on new shapes, and further new ideas may arise. What makes up the common ground of the symbolic order includes platitude, cliché, trampled ideas and worn out living. James Joyce's secretary, Samuel Beckett, could not imitate his mentor. He had to move away from Joyce's style, and Beckett did by moving in the opposite direction into uncharted territory, from effusion of language to minimalistic use of language. For certain, new ways of thinking about and writing are happening so that others may need time to find the logic in them or find the thread of the line of thought.

It is only through getting to know oneself and one's creative endeavors by way of solitude that the psychological concept of "flow" or what Maslow called peak experiences has meaning. That solitude allows one to also shepherd being, guide becoming without it being eaten by money making or other anxieties and distractions. It seems to me that peak experience probably comes long after what Malcolm Gladwell calls the 10,000 hours of practice that allows one to master his craft or field. When "mastery" is achieved one finds him/herself in the flow of his/her work that s/he has chosen for her/himself. While in that flow there are experiences that come now and again that break through flow to a new kind of flow. That break is the peak experience. This may be levels of achievement or inventing a new style of working and creating.

## SELF-ACTUALIZATION

How I got to this place where a new solitude lives within me is by way of practice and decades-long restlessness. The turf in which my poetry was embedded wasn't satisfying me. I was unhappy with the subjects I chose to write about as well as the way that I was writing about them. I had read that if an artist doesn't grow s/he parodies him/herself. It was my engagement with philosophy or the task of thinking in general that sprung me from the old turf, or at least gave me the illusion that I was springing from that turf. In my reading, I read Richard Rorty's *Contingency, Irony, and Solidarity*. Recognizing Wiggenstein's influence on Rorty's writing, I in turn was strongly influenced by "The method is to redescribe lots and lots of things in new ways, until you have created a pattern of linguistic behavior which will tempt the rising generation to adopt it, thereby causing them to look for appropriate new forms of nonlinguistic behavior..." Along with the following passages, I felt as though I was given permission (and how embarrassing for me because I prided myself in not needing permission from anyone).

> [R]evolutionary achievements in the arts, in the sciences, and in moral and political thought typically occur when somebody realizes that two or more of

> our vocabularies are interfering with each other, and proceeds to invent a new vocabulary to replace both. (*Contingency, Irony, and Solidarity* 1989: 12)

> We shall see the conscious need of the strong poet to *demonstrate* that he is not a copy or replica as merely a special form of an unconscious need everyone has: the need to come to terms with the blind impress which chance has given him, to make a self for himself by redescribing the impress in terms which are, if only marginally, his own. (*Contingency, Irony, and Solidarity* 1989: 22)

The idea of the strong poet not being a replica or creating imitations but redescribing the impress for himself by way of observing two vocabularies interfere with each other changed my way of looking at the poetry I was writing. While I could see Wittgenstein in the advice, I also saw an opportunity to perhaps help articulate or influence the language of the future. I assumed my role in the venture was, if not arrogant, then presumptuous but that was okay. That may be how it appears as an observer.

However, it is to be alone not simply in the writing but in the subjects and the style that is the result of the process. While it makes no promises, thinking without banisters has the ability to produce new lines of thought, new directions for whole cultures, or at least produces new language for old thinking. It can also be eccentric and not understood at all.

Though solitude can lead to breakdowns, especially if one isn't striving for self-actualization, Anthony Storr in his book *Solitude: A Return to the Self* suggests that "it is the struggle to give form and order to an external creative work that we also often without knowing it are imposing form and order on our mind... [M]aturation and integration can take place within the isolation" to a great extent (147). He goes on to suggest also that one may achieve "self-realization by self reference, that is, by interacting with their work rather than by interacting with other people." (147) So solitude can be a friend to the creative person, the fragile absolute on his/her path. The wound of our cosmic place that I received early and, perhaps due to it, my distrust of educational institutions, carried me into becoming so that I think to myself, "with enemies like these, who needs friends."

The attempt to define one's self and one's creative thinking is one where one breaks ties with one's past methods and style and the influences of colleagues and former influences. And it is a gamble with no promises. But as I like to remind myself, "we started as amoeba and got here by way of monkeys and will burn in the hell of the sun's explosive burn out. You don't have all that much to lose anyway." I can mumble that all I want, but the experience of approaching solipsism wears on the consciousness regardless. By the end of the day, I am hungry for conversation with a live person.

## SELF-REALIZATION AND THE DRIVE

On Youtube ("Personally Speaking: Conversations with Zygmunt Bauman"), an interviewer asked the thinker Zygmunt Bauman at age 92 what kept him going as a thinker and prolific writer. Bauman suggested that his watershed moment at 70 to leave sociological thinking and move on to more philosophical, ethical thinking. The challenge to oneself to grow fills oneself and is enough to satisfy each day that one has lived a life that more than he or she could have imagined at the start. That alone is enough. Yes, that kind of alone is enough. I imagine Zygmunt had projects that were left unfinished. He was the coyote chasing the Roadrunner off the cliff and doesn't realize that he is about to die. After a recent storm, a beautiful birch tree that was blown down was cut about three feet from the upended base and roots. The trunk had blocked the street so traffic couldn't pass. A week and more after the storm and the cut sap ran from the tree's exposed trunk, glistening in the sun. For me, the sap reminded me of Zygmunt. The sap for me is the projects left behind unfinished but promising, what has been called the excess of the death drive, the "I'm not done yet" of Zygmunt, a human being and a member of the fragile absolute of that I am certain.

My title "The Acts of a Solitary Thinker" is taken from something W. B. Yeats is supposed to have written about being a poet, so there is plenty of history behind thinking and writing alone. Perhaps the writer feels it more now that so little reading is being done other than the reading of text messages on a Smartphone. It may be that the greater engagement via virtual socialization within society exaggerates the writer's situation. I would imagine that the necessary isolation needed for writing and thinking will be very difficult for young people used to their eyes glued to a screen and fingers scrolling this way and that. To sit down and write when embedded in that heightened "social" experience of social media daily and knowing that very few will read your work has got to be difficult and painful for a young writer or artist. I suspect many will quit or not embark.

When one reads an anthology of dead poets, one reads unique poems by unique poets, not followers but poets striking out on their own without banisters which can win followers and at some point each of those followers either parodies him-or-herself or strikes out on his/her own. Growth leads to that divide in the road. Each poet makes the decision which way to go. I remember reading that Gary Snyder said something about poets reflect the culture of the age in which they write. There is truth to that, but if one finds that reflecting culture isn't enough and that the dice being thrown belong to someone else (and all is a throw of dice), then the poet packs his rucksack and heads for the psyche's undiscovered equivalent of Snyder's hideaway, Kitkitdizze.

## WORKS CITED

Arendt, Hannah. *Hannah Arendt: For the Love of the World.* Edited by Elisabeth Young-Bruehl. 2nd ed. New Haven: Yale University Press, 2004.

Bauman, Zygmunt. "Personally Speaking: Conversations with Zygmunt Bauman," Film 1. Dibb Directions. Electronic. 2017. https://www.youtube.com/watch?v=I9kmqx1-Slw.

Dostoevsky, Fyodor. Academy of Ideas. 2018. https://academyofideas.com/2017/08/psychology-of-solitude/

Gladwell, Malcolm. *Outliers.* New York: Little, Brown and Company, 2008.

Heidegger, Martin. "Letter on 'Humanism.'" *Pathmarks.* Edited by W. McNeil. Translated by Frank A. Capuzzi. Cambridge: Cambridge University Press, 1998.

Maslow, Abraham. Wikipedia entry. 2017. https://en.wikipedia.org/wiki/Abraham_Maslow.

Rorty, Richard. *Contingency, Irony, and Solidarity.* Cambridge: Cambridge University Press, 1989.

Sloterdijk, Peter. *You Must Change Your Life.* Translated by Wieland Hoban. Cambridge: Polity Press, 2013.

Storr, Anthony. *Solitude: A Return to the Self.* New York: Ballantine Books, 1989.

Žižek, Slavoj. *Less than Nothing*: *Hegel and the Shadow of Dialectical Materialism.* London: Verso, 2012.

We are in **Interregnum**, where **Capitalism is in Crisis,
Outside Plato's Cave,**
in a time when we can understand
**"The only truth is the inconsistent edifice of the logical interconnection of all possible illusion."** – Žižek
In need of
**Prophetic Voice Now,
A Cultural Climate Change.**
We may remember,
**"The fundamental job of the imagination in ordinary life,
then, is to produce, out of the society we have to live in,
a vision of the society we want to live in."** (Frye)
**Roads divide here as this poet's voice sees it.**
Teach children how to try live outside     or surrender to find oblivion in

<u>**To Praxis Makes;**</u>(Sloterdijk)         <u>**Plato's Cave**</u>

where in grade school children **Study Solace in Solitude** to balance the individual with the community learning to fail better;

Harari's **"Homo Deus"** is the shadow provider to Homo sapiens

where in high school each student is able to identify the individual **Hegelian Wound;**

who each experience Zuboff's **"Once I was mine; now I am theirs;"**

so that in college the student learns to **Mind Your Own Talent through Practice;**

and live Brown's **"All conduct is economic conduct"** until work is no longer possible for each

where **Life is lived in Over-Compensation Acrobatics** –with all the dialectical antagonisms;

and each is led to Conrad's **Grove of Death**, to where abandoned Homo sapiens withdraw to die.

and as a community **Fragile Absolute members reclaim the commons: Ecology, Biology, Public Spaces, Intellectual Property**(Žižek)

**"[A]nd thus it certainly does not pay to go up.** SOCRATES: And if they can get hold of this person who takes it in hand to free them from their chains and to lead them up, and if they could kill him, will they not actually kill him? GLAUCON: They certainly will."(Plato)

Epilogue

## Interregnum: Capitalism in Crisis

This epilogue is meant to explain the preceding image and to make clear to the reader what this writer understands as the stakes for democracy and humanity and add my voice to the prophetic voices that I hope may help change the direction of science and capitalism to one of a more human and commons-centered future. My prophetic offering merges Peter Sloterdijk's emphasis on routine and practice with Slavoj Žižek understanding of Freud's "death drive" to advocate for individuals practicing and mastering with overcompensation wounds or talents. As adults they would join in a community working to reclaim what is common and vital to every one of the practitioners as humans, Homo sapiens.

Zygmunt Bauman has called our current crisis of humanity an "interregnum" a contingent moment in modern cultures when there is no order among or within cultures and nations globally. His books *Liquid Modernity* and *Liquid Evil* define his term specifically and identifies in the latter TINA (there is no alternative) and the trigger to the "post-academic university . . . a blatant and blunt denial of the role of the humanities in modern society." (3) The liberal imagination and thought are found to be bankrupt, and general corruption is rampant. He continues: "The liquidity of evil signifies the divorce of the principle of imagination from the principle of reality." (5) He connects the crisis to a crisis in capitalism and we are experiencing his point. Slavoj Žižek concurs in *Less than Nothing* but identifies the moment as one outside Plato's cave, where "[t]he only truth is the inconsistent edifice of the logical interconnection of possible illusion." (11) In Plato's allegory a person alone finds his/her way to the sun and the reality. For Žižek the West and the whole world are in this moment outside the cave. According to Peter Sloterdijk he the book *You Must Change your life* as one who see the light of day and the book is a return to the cave with the news or explaining what needs to be done when at the mouth of the cave looking out.

For the West or world to be outside is one of fear, not only of the bright sun and the long acclimation to the reality of the day-to-day living in the open, but the lack of anchor or moral harbor for most people brings out the bestial animal qualities, the barbaric violence. Most people love the shadows where order and routine keep them reassured and passive and where decisions are made for them. If this is accurate, then one can understand how difficult democracy is for many people. But outside the cave or living interregnum is an opportunity to learn how to live outside it or to create a cultural climate change through narrative, through telling stories that lack scapegoats and guinea pigs. Even a softening of victimhood would be a better way than what the West and the world has achieved, an opportunity to bring a more responsible, less competitive second nature to being human.

The end of World War II up until the late 1960s brought great hope and vision for a more rational and emotionally intelligent West. There were leaders heralding the way, but were sacrificed on the altar of egalitarian change, scapegoats. The Kent State killings were intimidation. Leaders suggesting change away from the shadows in the cave are always at risk. These leaders all had a hard-won prophetic voice: John F. Kennedy, Martin Luther King, Malcolm X, and Robert Kennedy. However, their writings and the writings of others left a record of the possible, the potentiality for democratically minded readers today.

One such writer was Northrop Frye, a Canadian who saw what literacy and thinking could do for populations living in a democracy. He advocated the value of educating the imagination through reading literature. He understood that "[t]he fundamental job of the imagination in ordinary life, then, is to produce, out of the society we have to live in, a vision of the society we want to live it." (*The Educated Imagination*140) Joseph Brodsky went further: "[T]he social function of a poet is writing, which he does not by society's appointment but by his own volition. His only duty is to his language, that is, to write well. By writing, especially by writing well, in the language of his society, a poet takes a large step toward it. It is society's job to meet him halfway, that is, to open his book and to read it." (*On Grief and Reason* 205) He understood that it is through reading that a literate, imaginative, and thinking population safe-guards democracy. His was a prophetic voice.

It seems rational to promote the prophetic voice now while the influence of many voices singing may voice consensus in lyric or melody in an effort to shape a way forward. First, however the way forward that would only bring about stunted humans watching shadows on a cave wall must be voiced. The first of these threats to a stunted human for most people is what Yuval Noah Harari outlines in his book *Homo Deus*. His is a dystopian future where through artificial intelligence and genetic engineering that only the wealthy can afford will determine the future, where the rest of humanity is left behind to extinction. He warns that "once technology enables us to re-engineer human minds, Homo sapiens will disappear, human history will end." (53) Only a small percentage of humans would qualify for this vault into homo deus lives that live very long lives or forever, using the life sciences and AI to boost their kind. In fact, he states that even the Dataists are flanking from AI: "According to Dataism, human experiences are not sacred…Humans are merely tools for the-internet-of-all-things," a kind of God taking Zuboff's worry even further. (444)

The second threat to a greater humanity for all is what Shoshana Zuboff calls the coup from above where the Big Other directs every human behavior. Her book *The Age of Surveillance Capitalism: The Fight for a Human Future at the New Frontier of Power* describes in detail the threat of "an overthrow of people concealed as the technological Trojan horse that is the Big Other," where "every person except the tyrant is understood as an organism among organisms in an equivalency of Other-Ones." (513) In this dystopia once we were individuals responsible for thinking for ourselves and free to make choices that whether right or wrong could be used to learn from, we are seen as identical to every other as farmed animals. Zuboff also outlines in her conclusion how we, especially the young (who are babes in the woods) need to resist, to "be the friction" to surveillance in general and surveillance capitalism specifically.

The last threat to our way is "all conduct is economic conduct; all spheres of existence are framed and measured by economic terms and metrics" (10), what Wendy Brown's book explains as *The Undoing of Demos: Neoliberalism's Stealth Revolution*. In her book she describes how humans are conflated as human capital, where "any individual who veers into other pursuits risks impoverishment and loss of esteem and creditworthiness at the least, survival at the extreme." (22) She maps out how we got here and how the logic has infiltrated even higher education and healthcare and the way that politicians (Obama for instance) use the language of money over humans. She explains further: "Freedom conceived minimally as self-rule and more robustly as participation in rule by the demos gives way to comportment with a market instrumental rationality that radically constrains both choices and ambitions." (41) "[N]o longer is there an open question of how to craft the self or what paths to travel in life." (41)

These three dangers are either already arrived and need to be removed from a human life or are at the doorstep pounding at the door of a human future. There may be more radical or more emergency responses needed, especially considering that the threats ignore the threat of climate change. These forces alone but even more likely together could collapse the West, the world culture into an Easter Island phenomenon, an Atlantis for any surviving people.

Given that our global and national cultures are interregnum at this time and that we are at the threshold of such phenomena as the-internet-of-all-things and transhumans (or what Harari calls Homo Deus), giving voice to alternative myths (or ideologies) may help redirect the current direction. This epilogue offers an example, urging changing one's life through practice to become a member of Žižek "fragile absolute" in the struggle to reclaim the commons as space craft (Ecology, biology, intellectual property, etc.), referring to a place where humans value their being, their becoming, live as Nietzsche's acrobats in a global community minding its own talents. Žižek defines his term as "the community of believers qua "uncoupled" outcasts from the social order' clinging to 'the brief apparition of a future utopian Otherness."

However, a solution that changes the threat of Plato's cave to a more human oriented future is advocated by philosophers Peter Sloterdijk in his book *You Must Change Your Life* and in Žižek book *Less Than Nothing*. Sloterdijk advocates development of practice using as an example an armless violinist, Carl Hermann Unthan, in the late nineteenth century East Prussia who play at freak shows and in classical music venues, one in Budapest. Žižek calls this overcompensation the "Hegelian wound" bound to Freud's death drive that is the satisfaction beyond the pleasure principle. When the ideas of these two books are used as a lens to see how one might educate individuals and allow self-directed development, one sees how solidarity could be built of what Žižek would call the secular holy spirit and what might be also understood as a way to work together to take back the commons from the neoliberal capitalize everything.

An alternative, the practice that I lend my voice to is one of praxis in educating the imagination to re-open the humanities and humanity. I can envision that praxis would entail at least half of early childhood education and education in general from first grade through college. The societal effort would be one where we might resist the illusions of the cave or at least fail better. An effort from earliest years to old age would encourage each individual to understand the value of solitude and the value of community. Beginning with allowing individuals to respond to Hegelian wounds or born talents, the practitioners over-compensate into Übermensches even in old age, not a genetic and AI bolstered homo deus. The practice continually encourages each practitioner to reflect on their own becoming and struggle as members of the "fragile absolute" to reclaim the commons: Ecological commons, biological commons, public space commons, and intellectual property commons.

## WORKS CITED

Bauman, Zygmunt. *Liquid Evil*. Cambridge: Polity Press, 2016.
Brodsky, Joseph. "An Immodest Proposal," *On Grief and Reason*. New York: Farrar, Straus & Giroux, 1995.
Brown, Wendy. *The Undoing of Demos: Neoliberalism's Stealth Revolution*. Brookline: Zone Books, 2015.
Frye, Northrop. *The Educated Imagination*. Bloomington: Indiana University Press, 1964.
Harari, Yuval Noah. *Homo Deus: A Brief History of Tomorrow*. New York: Harper, 2016.
——. "Yuval Noah Harari and Steven Pinker in conversation," moderated by Dr. Maksyn Yakovlyev in September, 2019. www.youtube.com/watch?v=qHSzeijQ951.
Markovits, Daniel. *The Meritocracy Trap*. New York: Penguin Press, 2019.
Sloterdijk, Peter. *You Must Change Your Life*. Translated by Wieland Hoban. Cambridge: Polity Press, 2013
Žižek, Slavoj. *Less than Nothing: Hegel and the Shadow of Dialectical Materialism*. London: Verso, 2012.
Zuboff, Shoshana. *The Age of Surveillance Capitalism: The Fight for a Human Future at the New Frontier of Power*. New York: Public Affairs, 2019.

# Acknowledgements

Some of the individual chapters are based on previously published and presented work: "Vanishing Artist: American Poet and Differend," *The International Journal of the Humanities*, Vol. 1, issue 1 (2004); "McLuhan's Warning, Frye's Strategy, Emerson's Dream," *The Journal of the Assembly for Expanded Perspectives on Learning*, Vol. 12 (2006); "Spectacle and Aporia in Ted Kooser and John Ashbery," *Reconfigurations: A Journal of Poetry and Poetics*, Vol. 1 (2007). The essay appears with permission from Reconfigurations, where the work first appeared; "Poetry's Evolving Ecology: Toward a Post-Symbol Landscape," *The Journal of Ecocriticism*, *Poetic Ecologies* Special Issue (guest-edited by Franca Bellarsi), Vol. 1, No. 2 (pp. 131-140); "The Hopkins Path to Postmodern Poetry" *New Writing: The International Journal for the Practice and Theory of Creative Writing*, Volume 12, 2015 issue 3; "Reading Wisdoms," *New Writing: The International Journal for the Practice and Theory of Creative Writing*, Vol. 9 No. 3; "'Vexed to Nightmare by a Rocking Cradle': Ginsberg's Performativity," first experimental/exploratory version was presented as a paper at the 4th Annual Conference of the European Beat Studies Network that Franca Bellarsi co-convened with the EBSN at the *Université libre de Bruxelles* in 2015.

## *Author's Note*

I thank Tom Bourke for grasping Eliot, Baudelaire, and Shakespeare as though they were a battery pack to light up the modern era for me; George Starbuck and Derek Walcott for knowing the trajectory of my drive in language more clearly than I did; Bob Smart for recognizing that drive, for giving opportunity to it, and then for loving me as a brother; and literary editor and publisher Elizabeth Murphy for her expertise in bringing greater coherence and cohesion to the collection's appearance.

CPSIA information can be obtained
at www.ICGtesting.com
Printed in the USA
BVHW020851070621
608930BV00015B/385